Adrienne, 1967

Caneton en Papillote
La Petite Auberge

(for 4)

Sauce

Mince duck liver an equal amount of shallots, 6 cloves of garlic, pulverize thyme parsley, chervil, rosemary, oregano, savory [marjoram] etc. Mix all together and pass thru fine sieve. Add 1 spoon of strong white mustard, 1½ generous cups of dry white wine, 3½ ozs (¾ of a stick) of butter, melted, and 1 oz of beurre manié.

Mix all together — heat stirring constantly.

Correct taste by adding more herbs, salt pepper, beurre manié as needed.

———

Place spoon full of sauce on buttered paper place quarted (boned) duck on sauce — more sauce, cover with paper + secure — bake in moderate oven for 35 mins

Proportions of Herbs for
Caneton en Papillote

		Ratio 1 = ½ tsp.
Savory	7	– 3½ "
Thyme	18	– 9
Chervil	4	– 2
Rosemary	17	– 8½
Oregano	3	– 1½
Marjoram	5	– 2½
fresh Parsley	41	– 20½
Sage	5	– 2½

10 cloves of garlic
2½ cups white wine (or more?)
5½ oz butter
2 heaping teaspoons of butter beurre manié
½ cup livers
2/3 cup shallots
2 tspoon strong white mustard
1 Tblspoons of cassis ¾ – optional.
Salt + Pepper – Lots

Cooking with Adrienne

A Story of Friendship and Food

by
Joan M. Harper

For Michael,

Your love feeds my soul

And Martin,

Without you it could not have happened

ISBN #978-1539936077

Cover and illustrations by Kristina Wheeat and Anna Morozova

Harper Publications

Cheltenham, UK

There is no love sincerer
than the love of food.

— George Bernard Shaw

CONTENTS

Introduction

This book took over my life when my Best Foodie Friend, Adrienne, was diagnosed with a rare form of dementia* that would ultimately rob her of the ability to speak, write, and cook. We had been cooking together for over 20 years. In a panic, I realized that many of the recipes we had made were in her head and mine, or scribbled on bits of paper. In a race against time, I began writing down all of our recipes and as many stories as I could recall. The result is *Cooking with Adrienne.*

We were the most unlikely of friends. I was a small-town girl from Massachusetts with a penchant for eating dessert first. Adrienne grew up in Brooklyn, then lived and worked in Manhattan. She went to Europe on her honeymoon and came home with a duck press. I got married in 1980, honeymooned in New Jersey, and then moved to Queens. I began working as an account executive for an investor relations firm run by Adrienne's husband in 1984. That was my first bit of luck.

My second bit of luck came six years later when I had the good fortune to travel to Europe with Adrienne and her husband. For me it was business, but for them every trip they took was a food odyssey; their goal was to find and eat the best food on the planet. I never expected to get to London or Paris even once, much less travel to Europe regularly. And while the trips were a lot of work I wasn't complaining. I hadn't completed my bachelor's degree but I was communicating financial strategies, building relationships between corporate clients and the global investment community, and eating in pretty fancy places.

Over the next 20 years we dined at some of the greatest restaurants as well as wonderful holes-in-the-wall. The food changed me and my taste buds forever. I became a foodie. Which was a good thing because the rule on every trip with Adrienne was that you had to try everything put in front of you. There were no food prejudices allowed when eating with Adrienne. On the other hand we never wasted our calories on badly prepared food. If it wasn't good we left it over as a message to the chef.

My travels with Adrienne awakened my palate and made me want to cook at home the food that I had been eating abroad; I couldn't put the palate genie back in the bottle. However, I had two small children, a full time job, and no time to produce what I thought was the labor-intensive food that I had learned to love. That was when cooking with Adrienne really began. Despite my dessert-first culinary approach, Adrienne set to work educating my palate and teaching me to cook... anything and everything. I do wonder sometimes how I ended up living this life so far from where I began. But live it I did and still do.

The first thing Adrienne taught me was that all food is good food if properly prepared. And that making good, even great, food is within anyone's reach. It requires a bit of planning, a few basic skills, a willingness to taste everything, and an eye for presentation. A freezer full of homemade stock is also essential!

So who is Adrienne, and how did she become a doyenne of French cuisine? Like Gertrude Stein, Adrienne populated her life with the creative talents of her era. Her band of chefs from France included Gerard Boyer of Les Crayères; Alain Chapel of Chez La Mére Charles; Michel Guérard of les Prés d'Eugénie; Jean and Pierre Troisgros (and later Michel) of La Maison Troisgros; Roger Vergé of Moulin de Mougins; and, from Switzerland, Frédy Girardet of Restaurant Girardet. The food coming out of their kitchens revolutionized restaurant cuisine in the late sixties and throughout the seventies, resulting in nouvelle cuisine. Sadly, that term would later be hijacked by chefs with no clue what the revolution was about.

With Roger Vergé 1977

The "new" cuisine emphasized the quality and freshness of the ingredients; simplified the cooking and the accoutrements, including the sauce; and displayed the food on the plate in an artistic manner. Dining became a complete sensory experience, not just a means to an end. It was this type of food that beguiled me during my travels with Adrienne.

Adrienne honed her palate on this new cuisine with the insight and under the tutelage of the chefs creating it. She learned to re-create this food at home without the aid of kitchen staff and while keeping her day job as a financial portfolio manager. She became an accomplished cook, influenced by the new cuisine, but with her own distinctive style. She strongly believed that the act of cooking was an expression of love. Love of those for whom she was cooking, but also love of the process of transforming good raw materials into something great.

As the food revolution spread outwards from France in the seventies, Adrienne also became the facilitator for bringing these chefs and their new cuisine to America. Many had never been to the U.S. and were uncertain of the quality and availability of ingredients. Adrienne became their resource for locating products and food suppliers. In fact, many of these three-star chefs asked Adrienne to assist them in the kitchen or at the very least be on-site during cooking classes and demonstrations. Michel Guérard called Adrienne his *petite marmiton* when he taught a cooking class in Napa Valley for Robert Mondavi. Jean-Claude Vrinat, the owner of Taillevent in Paris, agreed to prepare a charity dinner at Tavern on the Green in New York City on the condition that Adrienne join his team. Jean and Pierre Troisgros would not accept any invitation to cook in America without vetting it with Adrienne and having her on-site.

With Jean Troisgros, Mondavi Kitchen, Napa Valley, 1978

By the time I was admitted to her kitchen, Adrienne had cooked dinner for four of the top chefs in France, all seated at the same table. They had 11 Michelin stars among them! What was it about Adrienne that made these chefs trust and value her? I think it was mostly two things: Adrienne had a sophisticated palate, and she was an incorrigible flirt. These two attributes alone were irresistible to most chefs. But she also thrived in a competitive work environment at a top investment bank, which was similar to the intensity experienced by many chefs in three-star kitchens. Indeed, many top chefs turned to her to manage their financial assets as their reputations grew.

In the beginning Adrienne was my mentor. Over the course of two decades our friendship grew. I was the skinny, blond, out-of-town *shiksa* to her sophisticated, wise-cracking New Yorker. She shared with me her recipes and stories of a life dedicated to cooking and eating the best food possible. She was an exacting teacher and I had constantly to earn my place in her kitchen. But the hours we spent side by side cooking, tasting, testing, and occasionally failing, were some of the happiest I have known.

Adrienne can no longer cook, write, or speak. Her voice is locked inside her head but her palate is still sharp and her mind continues to function. What's more, she can offer a critique or a compliment with a raised eyebrow or a sly grin. In this book I give you her best recipes and stories in the hope that they inspire you, as they did me, to find *joie de vivre* in kitchen.

A portion of the profits from Cooking with Adrienne will be donated to finding a cure for Primary Progressive Aphasia (PPA), also known as Pick's disease, which is the condition Adrienne is living with.

Auberge de l'Ill

In the Beginning

Cooking is like love. It should be entered into with abandon or not at all.

— Harriet van Horne

The first French phrase I learned was *tant pis* – pronounced *taun* (rhymes with "gone") *pee* – which generally translated means "Oh well," but it can actually mean many things, among them "who cares?" and "I want what I want!" The context for learning this phrase was on one of my first trips to France with Adrienne and her husband. We were sitting on the bank of the river at Auberge de l'Ill in Illhausern, perusing the menu. I didn't speak any French at the time but Adrienne was fluent, so she was doing all the ordering. As this was my first meal at Auberge de l'Ill, she wanted me to have the specialty of the house, which was Le Homard Prince Vladimir – sautéed lobster served in a Champagne sauce topped with crème fraîche. We were all having a salmon soufflé that sounded divine as a first course. Adrienne expected that the maître d'hôtel would recommend that the salmon was not the best thing for me to start with because both dishes were quite rich and had a cream-based sauce. If this transpired she would nod to me and I was to then speak my newly learnt phrase! It happened just

Les spécialités qui ont fait la renommée de l' Auberge de l' Ill

	Frs
Le potage de grenouilles au cresson	100
La terrine de foie gras truffee	210
La truffe sous la cendre	490
➤ Le saumon souffle "Auberge de 'l Ill"	170
La mousseline de grenouilles "Paul Haeberlin"	180
➤ Le homard Prince Wadimir	290

Les plats de la Cousine Bourgeoise et de notre terroir

La joue de boeuf braisée au Pinot Noir	160
et quenelles à la moelle	

as she predicted and after I uttered *"tant pis,"* the maître d'hôtel smiled graciously and wrote down the order exactly as it had been given.

This was an important lesson. Never let someone else tell you what or how to eat, not the maître d'hôtel of a three-star French restaurant or the writer of a cookbook. They may suggest, recommend, and advise, but if you want Lobster Prince Vladimir after salmon in a cream sauce, then you should have it.

It is the same with recipes. Each is meant as a framework, and where you go from there is the exciting part. If you want to jump to the Homard Prince Vladimir recipe, it is on page 90. But there are a few basic recipes you might want to get to grips with first.

The very first thing Adrienne taught me to make was a vinaigrette. In fact, it was a test to determine if our cooking friendship would progress. The reason it was so important is that creating an emulsion and tasting for the right amount of acidity are skills that form the foundation of every sauce and most of the recipes that we made together.

Homemade stock was the next thing I learned to make and is an essential ingredient for cooking. Walk into any good restaurant kitchen and the one thing you will always find is a pot of stock simmering on the stove. It doesn't require care or attention, just good bones, wine and aromatics. You will be rewarded many times over for the small effort required to make your own stock.

The basic sauces in this chapter are the ones that started me on the fascinating journey of learning how to add a flavor punch to simply cooked food.

My years cooking with Adrienne taught me that a well-stocked pantry and freezer are the keys to being able to cook almost anything. Having good oil, vinegar, and stock on hand, as well as access to fresh herbs, is the foundation of all cooking. See "In the Pantry" page 141, for more detail on what should be in your kitchen.

Vinaigrette – Making An Emulsion

To make a good salad is to be the perfect diplomat – the problem for both is to know how much oil one must put with one's vinegar.

— Oscar Wilde

A vinaigrette is a simple emulsion. You whisk the oil into the vinegar, not the other way around. It is about balance in taste and texture. The ability to create an emulsion is the basis for so many sauce recipes, from beurre blanc to hollandaise, so it is a valuable skill to master.

Balsamic vinegar should not be used in a vinaigrette, it is too heavy and sweet and will completely overwhelm most leaf salads. It is better used drizzled on vegetables or in the Summer Tomato Salad on page 56. Adrienne and I usually use vinaigre de Jerez (sherry vinegar) because it has a nice balance of acidity. The vinegar you use depends on the contents of the salad. If the ingredients are very rich, like avocado or blue cheese, you may want more acidity or a mixture of vinegars. The ratio of oil to vinegar is usually 3:1, but Adrienne liked to make her vinaigrette quite tart so she used 2:1. It's your vinaigrette so make it to your taste...*tant pis!*

You will probably need to experiment a few times with the Basic Vinaigrette recipe here (it took me five tries to get it right). Once you have mastered the emulsion, you can experiment with different combinations of vinegar and different types of oil. For example, walnut oil combined with white wine vinegar and just a drop of mustard to hold it all together works well on salads with blue cheese or apples in them. You can also make much larger quantities and store it in a jar in the fridge. You will never go back to buying salad dressing once you have made your own.

BASIC VINAIGRETTE

1 tablespoon sherry, red wine, or
   white wine vinegar
   (see Vinegar, page 143)

2 to 3 tablespoons best-quality
   extra virgin olive oil (see
   Butter and Oil, page 143)
1 teaspoon Dijon mustard

Pour the vinegar into a medium bowl deep enough to hold the completed vinaigrette and allow you to whisk effectively. Slowly drizzle in the oil, whisking all the time. Keep whisking until you have an emulsion that holds together. It will not stay emulsified, but taste it for the right balance of vinegar and oil. Add more oil if necessary. When you are happy with the emulsion, add a teaspoon of mustard, more or less to your taste. Taste again to insure the balance is correct. The mustard will help to hold the emulsion stable.

BOLD VINAIGRETTE

Adrienne and I became obsessed with the bright sharp taste of good French mustard. We used to fill up mustard pots at the Maille boutique in the Place de la Madeleine every time we were in Paris. The mustard was poured from barrels, much like beer is pumped from a tap, and then sealed with a cork. We would squirrel the pots away in our suitcases and look for reasons to lap the mustard up when we arrived back home. Fortunately, or not, you can now order Maille fresh "from the pump" mustard online or visit their boutiques in New York City, London, Brussels, or Sydney…but if ever you find yourself in Paris it is worth a visit.

When Adrienne found this bold vinaigrette recipe in the *New York Times* we knew it was a perfect use for that good strong French mustard. It is wonderful served on char-grilled vegetables or with a cold potato salad. The lemon juice is a nice addition because it has less acidity than vinegar, but adds the citrus tartness which works so well with vegetables. Because this recipe calls for so much mustard, the emulsion works best if you add the mustard with the vinegar and lemon juice and then whisk in the oil.

1 tablespoon freshly squeezed
   lemon juice
½ tablespoon red wine vinegar
5 tablespoons hot Dijon mustard

½ cup extra virgin olive oil
¼ teaspoon salt
Freshly ground black pepper

Whisk together the lemon juice, vinegar, and mustard. Slowly drizzle in the oil while whisking constantly. Season with salt and pepper.

Stock – The Basis for Sauce

Good stock will resurrect the dead.

— South American Proverb

1 n the depths of winter or on a gray autumn day, I would often find no less than three stockpots simmering away on the stove in Adrienne's kitchen. The aroma of the beef, chicken, or fish stock filled the kitchen and never failed to make me hungry.

No kitchen should be without good, homemade stock. In fact, it is a freezer full of stock that makes it possible to transform a simple dish into something elegant. Instead of smothering food with heavy cream and flour-based sauces, using stock in sauces helps to highlight the flavor of the food rather than masking it. It is also the classic example of the French housewife's motto, "never throw anything away," because it uses the uncooked beef, fish, or chicken bones that would otherwise go to waste. You can also use leftover bones from cooked chicken or meat, but the stock will not be as intense and the taste will be influenced by the cooking method and seasoning used. Stock made from uncooked bones is called white stock; stock made with cooked bones is called brown stock. Except for veal stock, the sauces in the book are made with white stocks. We store the bones in the freezer. When it is so full that nothing else will fit in, it is time to make stock.

Stock at its essence is an enriched broth made from bones, wine, aromatics, and seasoning. It is the go-to ingredient for sauces, stews, and soups and for deglazing a pan. You may think it is a lot of trouble and prefer to use plain broth or stock from a can, but I promise you that, just like with vinaigrette, once you make your own stock you won't go back to store-bought. In addition to its culinary uses, homemade stock is chock full of minerals like calcium, magnesium, phosphorus, and sulfur in a form that our bodies can easily absorb. The bones used to make stock also provide us with chondroitin and glucosamine, which many people now buy as supplements to support their own bones. Gelatin is another by-product that has proven to be helpful in treating digestive problems

Making stock requires only a few minutes to gather the ingredients, then let it simmer a few hours undisturbed. So pick a day when there isn't much to do outside, or set it to simmering while you make dinner. By the time you are done eating and have cleared the table your stock should be ready. Unless you are feeding an army, you will probably need to make a large batch of chicken stock two or three times a year. You can freeze it in 16-ounce containers. Beef, lamb, veal, and fish may be needed much less frequently, once or twice a year. If you don't have enough bones stored in your freezer, you can always request additional ones from your friendly butcher or fishmonger.

Most recipes for stock use water as the only liquid, but Adrienne always made her stock using commercially produced broth and good wine. This gives it a richer body which forms the base for many of her sauces. Always taste commercially made broth/stock before using it so you know how much seasoning to add to your own stock. As for the wine, cook with wine that is good enough to drink. Adrienne always used a young wine because it was very fruity and slightly more acidic than aged ones.

CHICKEN STOCK

Makes about 2¼ quarts

Prep/cook time: 3 hours

1½ to 2½ pounds uncooked bones, wing tips, and backbones from chicken, squab, or guinea fowl

48 ounces (6 cups) store-bought chicken broth or water (not cubes or powders, they're full of salt and preservatives)

2 to 3 cups dry white wine, such as a good Muscadet

1 onion, quartered

2 carrots, quartered

8 whole black peppercorns

1 stalk celery, cut in half

1 bouquet garni*

1 bay leaf

Combine all the ingredients in a large pot. Add water if the bones are not submerged. Bring to a boil. After 30 minutes reduce the heat so that the liquid is just simmering with a few bubbles forming. Cover and simmer for 2 hours. If the liquid reduces so that the bones and vegetables are showing through, add more water to cover. Remove from the heat and allow to cool.

Strain the stock through a sieve into a bowl, press on the solids to get out as much liquid as possible. Pour the stock into containers and allow to cool completely before covering, labeling, and freezing. Mark the date on the container and note any particular ingredients.

* See page 146

BEEF OR LAMB STOCK

Makes about 2¼ quarts

Prep/cook time: 3 hours

1½ to 2½ pounds beef <u>or</u> lamb bones (do not combine)

48 ounces (6 cups) store-bought beef broth* or water

2 to 3 cups red wine, a Côtes du Rhône works well

1 onion, quartered

2 carrots, quartered

8 whole black peppercorns

1 celery rib, cut in half

1 bouquet garni**

1 bay leaf

Combine all ingredients in a large pot. Add water to cover if the bones are not submerged. Bring to a boil. After 30 minutes, reduce the heat so that the liquid is just simmering with a few bubbles forming. Cover and simmer for 2 hours. Remove from heat and allow to cool.

Strain the liquid through a sieve into a bowl get out as much liquid as possible. Pour the stock into containers and allow to cool completely before covering, labeling, and freezing. Mark the date on the container and note any particular ingredients.

---

* Since lamb broth is not commercially available, you can use beef broth for both beef and lamb stock; but don't use cubes or powders - they have too much sodium and preservatives.

** See page 146

DEMI-GLACE AND GLACE DE VIANDE

Concentrated Veal Stock

Veal stock adds a mysterious richness to sauces. It is often the secret ingredient missing from many restaurant recipes when they are published. Adrienne often added some to her fish sauces for a wonderful silkiness and depth. This is Michel Guérard's recipe, which results in a concentrated stock called demi-glace. You roast the bones first and then simmer the stock on top of the stove for 6 to 7 hours, when all you need to do is top up the water occasionally. Reduced even further and you have *glace de viande.*

Makes about 3 cups demi-glace or scant 1 cup glace de viande

Prep time: 1½ hours Cook time: 6 to 9 hours

2 pounds veal shank bones (not for osso buco), cut into sections 1 to 2 inches long

Sunflower oil

1 to 2 tablespoons unsalted butter

1 carrot, peeled and diced

1 medium onion, chopped

4 scallions, chopped

1½ cups dry white wine, such as Muscadet

1 teaspoon salt

½ teaspoon dried thyme

4 sprigs fresh Italian flat-leaf parsley

1 bay leaf

Preheat the oven to 450°F. In a roasting pan, toss the veal bones with a small amount of sunflower oil. Roast, turning the bones after 25 minutes, for about 50 minutes total, until browned but not burnt.

Heat 1 tablespoon of butter in a large heavy pot and sauté the carrot, onion and scallions until the carrot is softened and shiny and the onion is translucent. Add the veal bones. If the vegetables have absorbed all the butter, add an additional tablespoon. Cover and cook over very low heat for 15 minutes.

continued

Add ½ cup of wine, raise the heat to high, and cook uncovered for about 10 minutes, until the liquid evaporates and the meat juices in the bottom of the pot turn brown; don't let them burn. Repeat this process twice with ½ cup of wine each time; this builds the flavor and produces a rich veal stock.

Cover the contents of the pot with hot water and bring to a boil. Add salt, thyme, parsley and bay leaf. Reduce the heat and simmer uncovered for 5 to 6 hours, adding additional water to keep the bones covered at all times. Strain the stock, cool to room temperature, and refrigerate for a few hours or overnight. You will have about 3 cups demi-glace. Skim off the layer of fat that forms on the top before freezing or using.

To make *glace de viande*, return the stock to the pot after removing the fat. Bring to a boil until reduced by two-thirds, approximately 1 to 2 hours. You will have a scant cup of quite viscous glace de viande. Recipes usually call for a tablespoon or two of glace de viande so if you are planning to freeze it, first pour the finished stock into a baking dish and allow it to gel in the fridge. Cut it into 3-inch squares and freeze in plastic bags. Or you can freeze it in plastic ice cube trays, then pop the cubes into plastic bags and return to the freezer.

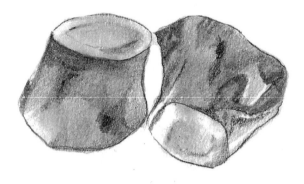

FISH STOCK

Adrienne always made her fish stock with water, because it was almost impossible to get good fish broth commercially. Many supermarkets and fishmongers are beginning to carry it now, but your stock will be just as good as Adrienne's if you use water and wine.

Makes about 4 cups

Prep/cook time: 60 to 90 minutes

2 whole cloves

1 onion, halved

3 to 4 fish skeletons and/or heads (not from oily fish like salmon or bluefish; otherwise anything goes)

2 carrots, peeled and chopped into chunks

2 stalks celery, quartered

A few branches fresh Italian flat-leaf parsley

1 bay leaf

2 large cloves garlic, peeled

3 sprigs fresh thyme

8 to 10 whole peppercorns

1 tablespoon coarse (kosher or sea) salt

About 4 cups water and/or fish broth

1 bottle (750ml) white wine, such as Muscadet or other dry white wine

Insert one clove into each onion half. Put all ingredients in a stockpot except the water and wine. Add enough water or broth and water to just cover the ingredients. Bring to a boil, reduce the heat, and simmer for 20 minutes. Add about 2½ cups of the wine and simmer for an additional 40 minutes. Taste. If you are making the stock to have in reserve, I would stop here.

If you want a stronger fish taste for a sauce or bouillabaisse, simmer 10 to 15 minutes longer. If you want a richer, fuller taste, add the rest of the wine and boil vigorously for an additional 15 minutes. Remember this is fish stock, not chicken stock, so it is not going to have big taste. And it is not a sauce yet, but has the potential to become one.

continued

Strain the stock through a sieve, pressing hard on the solids. Cool to room temperature. Refrigerate for up to a week or freeze for up to a year.

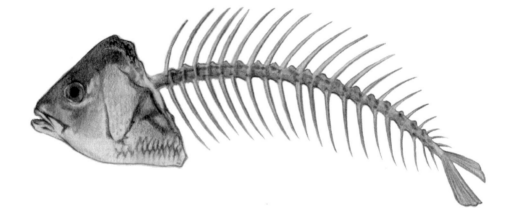

SHELLFISH STOCK

One summer when the lobsters were abundant and cheap, my freezer filled up with all the shells (never throw anything away!) so we had to make shellfish stock. It is the base for the Provençal Halibut on page 84 and it can also be used to make fish soup or bisque.

The shells of the cooked lobsters need to be cracked to release the flavor. But don't do what Adrienne did the first time she made this. She put the shells in the Cuisinart, thinking it would be faster than cracking them with a mallet. The shells destroyed the plastic bowl and the blade!

Makes about 4 cups

Prep/cook time: 90 minutes

3 or 4 medium lobster shells, cracked into rough pieces

Olive oil

2 medium carrots, quartered

1 stalk celery, cut in half

1 shallot, peeled and quartered

8 whole black peppercorns

1 bay leaf

1 branch fresh tarragon

1 sprig fresh thyme

4 cups Fish Stock (page 27)

2 cups white wine

2 cups water

Preheat the oven to 300°F. Place the lobster shells in a baking pan, sprinkle with olive oil, and bake for 30 minutes, until dark red but not burned.

Transfer the shells to a stockpot. Add the carrots, celery, shallot, peppercorns, bay leaf, tarragon, and thyme. Combine the stock, wine, and water in a large bowl. Add enough of the stock mixture to the pot to cover the ingredients, adding additional water if necessary. Bring to a boil and simmer for 1 hour, until the liquid is reduced by half. Cool to room temperature, strain, and freeze for up to a year.

COURT BOUILLON

Court bouillon is simply a broth for poaching fish. This is André Soltner's recipe which is very easy to make. You can store it in the fridge for a few weeks or the freezer for up to three months.

Makes 2 quarts

Prep/cook time: 45 minutes

2 quarts water
½ cup white wine vinegar or tarragon vinegar
1 leek, washed and sliced
4 stalks celery, cut into quarters
1 medium onion, cut into eighths
½ teaspoon freshly ground black pepper
Grated zest of ½ lemon
Grated zest of ½ orange
1 tablespoon sea salt
1 bay leaf
1 sprig fresh thyme
2 cloves garlic, halved
1 cup dry white wine

Combine all ingredients except the wine in a large stockpot. Bring to a boil and simmer for 15 minutes.

Add the wine and simmer for an additional 15 minutes.

Remove from the heat. Do not strain. Use immediately for poaching fish or pour into containers and refrigerate or freeze.

Sauce – The Magic Revealed

A well-made sauce will make an elephant or even a grandfather palatable.

— Grimod de la Reynière

Adrienne was the Queen of Sauce. She made old-fashioned sauces like bordelaise, Amoricaine, and Périgueux, as well as new-fashioned ones like Riesling sabayon and sorrel sauce for salmon. But Adrienne was at her best and most inspired when she created a sauce out of her head. Or should I say, out of her taste buds, because that is where it all started. She would have a sense of the taste she wanted and would start by reducing stock and adding wine, vinegar, herbs, and spices. Then she would add the Secret Ingredient. And I am going to tell you exactly what that Secret Ingredient is so that you too can make amazing sauces.

Adrienne took the French housewife's mantra, "never throw anything away," to the extreme when it came to sauce. Every time she made a sauce she froze every last unconsumed bit so that the next time she made something similar she would have that Secret Ingredient to add the finishing touch to a sauce. Her freezer was full, as mine is today, of a repertoire of sauces in dozens of jars labeled "great rosemary chicken sauce" or "very rich morille sauce." You may think that this is a bit obsessive and you would be right. But this little bit of effort will reward you many times over. Though you may have to buy a bigger freezer!

Sorrel Sauce (page 48) is always in my freezer. It has a lemony taste that is perfect on salmon, but can also be used on a variety of simply grilled fish and even chicken. It turns a Tuesday night dinner into something special. The Sauce Batârde (page 42) has so many uses that, while it can't be frozen, it won't stay in your fridge long enough to spoil. It is wonderfully easy to make and delicious on asparagus, scallops, or the classic poached egg. And finally, Beurre Blanc (page 44) – many a cook's nemesis. But I promise, if you can make a vinaigrette, you can make a beurre blanc.

But before we get to these essential sauces, let's start with the basic building blocks for a sauce. A sauce starts with everything that comes out of cooking a piece of meat, chicken, or fish. The drippings and browned bits that form during the cooking process contain the essence of what you have cooked. The trick is getting them loose from the pan you have cooked them in. Usually it is a simple process of deglazing the pan with stock or wine. Over medium to high heat, pour in a cup or two of wine – white or red depending on what you have cooked – it will hiss and steam which is what it should do. That will help loosen the good bits that are stuck to the pan as you scrape with a wooden spoon.

I prefer to use the wine to deglaze and then add the stock as an enrichment rather than letting it evaporate during the deglazing. You should never waste a drop of pan drippings or juice, unless they are burnt or have an unpleasant taste. The drippings from a roast leg of lamb for example will not be very appealing because of the taste of the lamb fat. But you can still make a lovely sauce using lamb stock (see page 24).

Having good stock (see pages 21 to 30) in your freezer is the next essential ingredient. The recipe for Beurre manié (page 35) is the final ingredient you need to make your sauces silky smooth. A mixture of equal parts butter and flour is kneaded together to make a paste. A small amount added to a sauce or stew will bind it together and give it an unctuous quality without a floury taste.

When you understand the framework for making a sauce, you can begin experimenting with tastes and different ingredients. Just remember that the wine or stock is used at the beginning to deglaze and enrich. Additional wine can be added later, but must cook with the sauce. The beurre manié is added towards the end and must cook for 10 to 15 minutes before serving. Other ingredients are added depending on how much cooking they need. The idea is that you build up the tastes in the sauce with each ingredient. The longer you simmer the stock and wine with the pan drippings, the more intense the flavor. But there is a point at which the liquid will turn syrupy – essentially caramelized. This can be corrected by adding more stock. There are those who think this intense reduction complements a dish. In most cases I think it overwhelms it so that the sauce becomes the focus, not the meat or fish. Sauce should dress the dish, add flavor, and, in some cases, provide a counterbalancing taste to the main course.

In the summer we often grilled outdoors so there wouldn't be any juice or drippings to make a sauce. In that case, Adrienne whipped up a quick sauce by boiling 2 cups homemade stock with a ½ cup wine until reduced by half. Then she would add any of the additions from the recipes here – vinegar/lemon juice, cream/crème fraîche, herbs, tomatoes, mushrooms, or shallots – depending on what was being served. She would finish with the beurre manié .

Remember to taste as you go, even if you have made a sauce ten times, as it will be slightly different every time. Tasting as you go is a crucial step in every recipe, but critically important when building a sauce. In fact, I think tasting a dish or sauce at every point in the cooking process is the one skill that builds your palate and your confidence in the final result.

A WORD ABOUT VINEGAR

There are a multitude of different vinegars in my pantry. And every time I come across a new one I taste it and often buy it. On a recent trip to the Languedoc, France, on a road in the Midi-Pyrenees, we stopped at a shop which was miles from any town. There I tasted a vinegar made from honey which was surprising for its agro dolce (tart/sweet) quality. I brought it home without any certainty of how I would use it. Then one day I sprinkled it on some rather tasteless winter cherry tomatoes and stuck them in the oven to roast. What came out was a lovely explosion of flavor.

Adrienne's frequent use of vinegar surprised me at first, but I quickly became a convert. Think of vinegar as a seasoning, like salt or pepper; it is that essential to cooking. Almost every meat braise can benefit from a dash of red or white wine vinegar. Vegetable braises like ratatouille cry out for something to cut the sweetness that occurs when vegetables are slow cooked. You don't want to add too much, just enough to brighten and cut the sweetness.

When it comes to making a sauce, vinegar or lemon juice is almost always the last adjustment to taste, along with the salt and pepper. This is why it is important to have a variety of vinegars on hand – see the section on Vinegar (page 143).

The use of vinegar in cooking and the necessity of tasting as you go are the core lessons of my years cooking with Adrienne. There is much, much more in this book, but if you take nothing else away except these two elements, you will be a better cook.

BEURRE MANIÉ

Kneaded Butter

This is one of the best tricks for finishing a sauce. When you want to thicken a sauce, pan juices, or stew, you usually add a small amount of flour and/or butter. The problem with incorporating the flour is that it inevitably forms lumps. Corn starch and arrowroot are easier to incorporate, but can still result in lumps and sometimes affect the taste. Beurre manié is a paste of equal parts flour and butter which you whisk into your sauce about 15 minutes before serving, allowing the flour to "cook" and bind to the butter, which adds richness without lumps.

You can double or triple the recipe so that you always have a supply on hand. Roll it into a log and freeze it; it will keep for up to six months. When you start making your sauce, cut off a chunk. It will be thawed and ready to use in time to finish the sauce.

1 tablespoon all-purpose flour

1 tablespoon unsalted butter, at room temperature

Place the flour and butter on a piece of plastic wrap and knead the two together until you have a smooth paste.

To use, remove your sauce from the heat and whisk in the beurre manié. You dont need much. Start off with a small piece the size of a marble and whisk it in; the sauce will thicken more after the beurre manié is cooked. Put the pan back on medium heat and simmer for 10 to 15 minutes to cook the flour.

JUS LIÉ

White Wine Sauce

This is the first proper sauce I made under Adrienne's guidance. A jus lié is a simple reduction of cooking juices (jus) and works perfectly with quickly sautéed chicken breasts or fish fillets.

If you'd like to steam chicken or fish in foil, rather than sautéing, pour the juices from the foil into the saucepan along with a tablespoon of butter and proceed with adding the stock and ½ cup white wine.

The optional cherry tomatoes work well with both chicken and fish.

Makes about 1 cup

Prep/cook time: 30 minutes

1 cup white wine

½ to ¾ cup Chicken Stock (page 23) or Fish Stock (page 27)

1 branch fresh rosemary, thyme, or tarragon

1 to 2 tablespoons white wine vinegar, Champagne vinegar, or freshly squeezed lemon juice

Salt and freshly ground black pepper

1 to 2 teaspoons Beurre Manié (page 35)

10 cherry tomatoes, halved, optional

After sautéing chicken or fish, remove it from the sauté pan and place on a warm, covered plate. Pour off most of the fat from the pan but don't get too crazy about it. Return the pan to medium-high heat and pour in the white wine. It will bubble and hiss, which is good. Stir it with a wooden spoon to get up all the crispy bits from the chicken or fish.

Add ½ cup stock and the branch of rosemary (for chicken) or thyme or tarragon (for fish). Boil for about 10 minutes, until the liquid reduces by half - the more you reduce, the more intense the flavor. If it reduces too much, add the additional ¼ cup stock and simmer gently. Taste.

Add 1 tablespoon vinegar or lemon juice and season with salt and pepper. Simmer for a few minutes and taste. If the sauce is a bit sweet or not vibrant enough, add the second tablespoon of vinegar or juice and simmer again.

Remove from heat and whisk in 1 teaspoon beurre manié. Return to the heat and allow to simmer for 10 minutes. If the consistency is not to your liking, repeat with another teaspoon beurre manié and simmer again for 10 minutes.

Once you have the consistency right, you can remove the herb branch and serve; or add the cherry tomatoes and simmer for 5 more minutes. Taste and correct seasoning – add salt, pepper, vinegar/lemon juice as needed. Do not add more wine. Wine, in most cases, should be cooked into a sauce, adding more than a tablespoon or two at the end before serving will make it taste sour. But do add any of the juices exuded from the chicken or fish while it has been resting.

SAUCE SUPRÊME

Basic Cream Sauce (for Chicken or Fish)

A sauce suprême traditionally starts with a velouté made with chicken stock, flour, and butter, to which you add the cream or crème fraîche and mushrooms. This lighter quicker version eliminates the velouté and is essentially a jus lié with cream and mushrooms added. But there is no name for that, so we always called it sauce suprême.

Makes about 1 cup

Prep/cook time: 45 minutes

10 white or brown button mushrooms, quartered

2 to 3 tablespoons unsalted butter

Fresh thyme sprig, optional

Salt and freshly ground black pepper

1 cup white wine

1 shallot, finely chopped, optional

½ to ¾ cup Chicken Stock (page 23) or Fish Stock (page 27)

1 branch fresh Italian flat-leaf parsley, plus additional chopped parsley for garnish

Squeeze of lemon or dash of vinegar

⅓ cup cream or crème fraîche

1 teaspoon Beurre Manié (page 35), if needed

In a sauté pan, heat 2 tablespoons butter to foaming over medium-high heat. Add the mushrooms and a sprig of thyme. When the mushrooms have absorbed the butter, about 5 minutes, leave them to cook over low heat until they begin to exude some of their liquid. Season with salt and pepper. Do not add more butter. When they are slightly brown on the edges, 10 to 15 minutes, deglaze with ¼ cup of the white wine and set aside but keep warm.

After sautéing chicken or fish, remove it from the sauté pan and place on a warm, covered plate. Add the shallot to the pan and cook over medium heat, adding a tablespoon of butter if necessary, until translucent but not colored. Pour in the remaining ¾ cup wine. It will bubble and hiss, which is good. Stir with a wooden spoon to get up all the crispy bits from the chicken or fish. Add ½ cup stock and the branch of parsley. Simmer over medium-high heat for 10 minutes, until the liquid reduces by half (the more you reduce, the more intense the flavor). If it reduces too much, add an additional ¼ cup stock and simmer gently. Taste. Add a dash of vinegar or lemon juice, and salt and pepper. Simmer for a few minutes and taste.

Remove the parsley branch. Off the heat, whisk in the cream or crème fraîche. Return to the heat and simmer for a few minutes. Add the mushrooms. Taste and correct seasoning. You may need freshly ground pepper and another squeeze of lemon juice to cut the richness of the cream. You may also need the beurre manié, but don't add it unless the sauce is very thin and be sure to simmer for 10 minutes to cook the flour. Sprinkle with chopped parsley.

If you are afraid of butter, use cream.

— Julia Child

SAUCE DUXELLES

Red Wine Sauce with Mushrooms

Makes about 1 cup

Prep/cook time: 30 minutes

10 brown button or portobellini mushrooms, quartered

2 tablespoons unsalted butter

Sprig fresh thyme, optional

Salt and freshly ground black pepper

1 cup red wine, a Côtes du Rhône works well

½ to ¾ cup Chicken Stock (page 23), or Lamb or Beef Stock (page 24)

1 branch fresh thyme or rosemary

1 to 2 tablespoon sherry vinegar or red wine vinegar

1 to 2 teaspoons Beurre Manié (page 35)

In a sauté pan, heat the butter to foaming over medium heat. Add the mushrooms and sprig of thyme. When they have absorbed the butter, about 5 minutes, leave them to cook over low heat until they begin to exude some of their liquid. Season with salt and pepper. Do not add more butter. When they are slightly brown on the edges, 10 to 15 minutes, deglaze the pan with ¼ cup of the red wine. Set aside.

After sautéing chicken, lamb, or beef, remove from the pan and place on a warm, covered plate. Pour off most of the fat from the pan but don't get too crazy about it. Return the pan to medium-high heat and pour in the remaining ¾ cup wine. It will bubble and hiss, which is good. Stir with a wooden spoon to get up all the crispy bits from cooking the meat. Add ½ cup stock and the branch of rosemary or thyme. Simmer for about 10 minutes, until the liquid reduces by half (the more you reduce, the more intense the flavor). If it reduces too much, add an additional ¼ cup stock and simmer gently. Taste. Add a tablespoon of vinegar, and salt and pepper to taste. Simmer for a few minutes and taste. If the sauce is a bit sweet or not vibrant enough, add the second tablespoon of vinegar and simmer again.

Remove from heat and whisk in 1 teaspoon beurre manié. Return to heat and allow to simmer for 10 minutes. If the consistency is not to your liking, repeat with another teaspoon beurre manié and simmer again for 10 minutes. Once you have the consistency about right, remove the rosemary or thyme branch and add the mushrooms and simmer for 5 more minutes. Taste and correct seasoning as needed. Do not add more wine. Wine, in most cases, should be cooked into a sauce, so adding more than a tablespoon or two at the end before serving will make it taste sour. But do add any of the juices exuded from the meat while it has been resting.

SAUCE BATÂRDE

Mock Hollandaise

Adrienne made this one evening on the spur of the moment when we were having a simple dinner of grilled scallops and a salad. I love the bright lemony lightness of it and the fact that it can be used on so many different dishes: Try it on trout with a bit of dill chopped in at the end, or any other fish, chicken, boiled potatoes, asparagus, or even on eggs Benedict. It is essentially a hollandaise without all the trouble, and more stable due to the addition of the flour. You can store it in the fridge for up to two weeks. Unlike the Beurre Blanc (page 44), it can be gently reheated; but don't use a microwave or it will separate.

I call it Sauce Batârde but that is not exactly correct because an authentic batârde uses chicken or fish stock and in this recipe we use lemon juice. You can easily substitute ½ cup stock for the lemon juice depending on what you are serving. In that case, you may want to add a squeeze of lemon at the end before the final butter.

Makes 1½ cups

Prep/cook time: 25 minutes

6 to 8 tablespoons (¾ to 1 stick) unsalted butter	1 cup white wine
	Juice of 1 lemon
1 tablespoon finely chopped shallot	2 egg yolks
	1 teaspoon Dijon mustard
2 tablespoons all-purpose flour	Salt and freshly ground pepper

Melt 2 tablespoons of the butter in a saucepan over medium heat. Add the shallots when the butter is foaming and cook for 2 to 3 minutes – don't let it brown. Add the flour and blend into a smooth paste. Add the wine and allow to simmer for 5 to 6 minutes, until the sauce has a smooth consistency. Stir in the lemon juice and remove from heat.

In a medium bowl, blend the egg yolks and mustard with a wire whisk. Measure out ½ cup of the hot liquid from the saucepan. Add the liquid, a teaspoon at a time, to the egg yolk mixture, whisking after each addition. When you have added 3 teaspoons, whisk the rest in a thin stream (this acclimatizes the egg to the temperature of the liquid, preventing it from scrambling). Pour the egg mixture back into the saucepan and simmer until it has thickened slightly, about 5 minutes. Taste for seasoning – it will probably need salt and pepper – use white pepper if you have it. Keep warm over very low heat until ready to serve. Just before serving, remove from the heat and beat in 4 to 6 tablespoons softened butter – depending on taste and consistency.

BEURRE BLANC

White Butter Sauce

Even experienced home chefs cringe at the thought of making a beurre blanc, as I did. The first time I made it, I didn't have Adrienne by my side coaching me; I was on my own in my kitchen in New Jersey. We didn't start cooking together properly until I moved to Long Island in 1994. But she assured me if I could make a vinaigrette, which I could, then I could make a beurre blanc. So on a weekend night when my kids were with their dad, I took a deep breath and said, "*Tant pis*, I will make a beurre blanc!"

A beurre blanc is a warm emulsion, rather than a cold one (such as a vinaigrette). The warmth keeps the milk solids in the butter suspended. Too much heat will cause the emulsion to separate into solids and oily clarified butter. But, thanks to Adrienne and Julia Child, I discovered it is easy to hold it over a very, very low heat while you finish cooking the rest of the meal and then dribble in a few tablespoons of very hot cream before serving. Do not to try to heat it up once you have it emulsified or it will be ruined and nothing, but nothing, will restore it.

Most cookbooks tell you that you cannot re-use beurre blanc but that's not true. You cannot reheat it; but if you refrigerate any leftover sauce, it will solidify since it is mostly melted butter. When you want to use it again, remove it from the fridge and allow it to come to room temperature. Scoop out a spoonful and dollop it on hot fish or vegetables. It will melt and no longer be completely emulsified but it will taste delish.

You can use beurre blanc on almost any fish. It is also particularly good on fresh young asparagus. This recipe is not much changed from the one in Julia Child's *Mastering the Art of French Cooking*, which Adrienne gave me in 1993 and has been my go-to reference for all things sauce. Adrienne always used vermouth, but white wine or lemon juice works just as well.

Makes 1 cup

Prep/cook time: 30 minutes

2½ tablespoons white wine vinegar

2½ tablespoons vermouth, white wine, or freshly squeezed lemon juice

1 tablespoon finely minced shallot

Salt and white pepper

2 tablespoons unsalted butter; plus 1 cup (2 sticks) cold unsalted butter, cut into 16 pieces

Freshly squeezed lemon juice

In a saucepan, simmer the vinegar, vermouth, shallot, ½ teaspoon salt, ⅛ teaspoon pepper, and the 2 tablespoons butter until reduced to approximately 1½ tablespoons, about 5 minutes.

Remove the saucepan from the heat and immediately whisk in 2 pieces of the cold butter. As the butter softens and creams into the liquid, beat in another piece. Set the saucepan on very low heat. Continue whisking in successive pieces of butter as the previous one has almost creamed into the sauce until all the butter is incorporated. The sauce will be thick and ivory colored. Immediately remove the pan from the heat and taste. It will need more salt and pepper and perhaps a squeeze of lemon.

To keep the sauce warm until you are ready to serve, cover the pan and place it near a warm burner or pilot light, but not over direct heat; or set it over barely warm water. Stir it occasionally to ensure that it doesn't separate. If it is not hot enough when you are ready to serve it, dribble a tablespoon or two of hot cream into the sauce to raise the temperature. Remember you will be serving it on hot food, so the sauce itself does not need to be piping hot.

THE TROISGROS FAMILY

Adrienne with Pierre and Jean Troisgros in Roanne June 1973

In January 1969 Adrienne and her husband arrived at Restaurant Frères Troisgros in Roanne having heard whispers about the food the brothers Jean and Pierre were producing. It was a rustic looking restaurant across from the train station and at the time catering mostly to locals. However, the food the Troisgros brothers were preparing in their humble kitchen was beginning to be recognized as "nouvelle." Upon arriving, Adrienne asked to see the chef in order to discuss the menu. Jean emerged from the kitchen and after working out a menu they then consulted the wine list. When Adrienne's husband selected the wines Jean seemed to be in a bit of a panic and brought Pierre out of the kitchen. The two had a lively discussion in French and announced that they had completely changed the menu because the wines were far too good for the original dishes. That was the beginning of a friendship which grew into a lifelong bond with the entire Troisgros family.

DINNER JANUARY 1969
Restaurant Frères Troisgros

Adrienne made notes during and after every restaurant meal they ate while traveling in Europe beginning in 1965. Here are her notes and ratings of the dishes from their first meal at Troisgros. See page 87 for more details on her rating system.

Pâté de foie gras and **pâté de grives** 2*

Tourte en feuillete sauce Bordelaise – a meat pie with nice demi-feuillete pastry, scrambled egg-like custard and quite spicy veal or duck filling; the sauce was very thick and highly peppered, a marvelous new taste combination. 3*

Cold écrevisses salad served on a bed of chopped lettuce and covered in mustard mayonnaise in which some écrevisses coral had been mixed – very nice taste and texture, the écrevisses very succulent but the dish was too mundane.

Escalope de Saumon frais crème a l'Oseille – I was in ectasy over the exquisite taste of the salmon and the blending of the taste of the salmon with the delicacy and acidity of the sauce. Martin, who was eating the same dish, looked at me as if I were nuts. It was the first time I'd ever had salmon cooked rare and that is when it clicked into place. My escalope was thicker and slightly undercooked compared with his. The difference it made is hard to credit. Mine 3* His 1*

Salmis de Becasse – very strong sauce, not gamy, delicious and the becasse was very tender and juicy completely 3*

Fromage – quite good, one creamy chevre the best we'd had yet.

Sorbet Ananas – excellent with fantastic crème fraiche and served with jus de framboise on top.

Wine: Blagny, Hospice de Beaune Jos. Matrot 1961 – excellent
Clos de Vougeot Domaine Henri Lamarch 1955

SAUCE L'OSEILLE

Sorrel Sauce

This is a classic Adrienne sauce, full of delicate acidity yet luscious – rather like Adrienne herself! It is based on the Jean Troisgros signature dish, Saumon au l'Oseille, which is still served at the eponymous three-star La Maison Troisgros in Roanne, France. The lemony tartness of the sorrel provides a surprising contrast to salmon. This is an incredibly versatile sauce and one that I always have in the freezer. It works equally well with any strong tasting, firm fish or even chicken that has been simply sautéed. The sauce turns a simple dish into something sublime.

It is essential to have good homemade fish stock because it is the backbone of the sauce. The sorrel leaves "melt" into the sauce very quickly so you don't cook them, you add them to the sauce at the end to release their flavor just before serving. The sauce should be rich from the reduced fish stock and cream, and a bit lemony but not acidic, before you add the sorrel. When you reheat the sauce you should add a few squeezes of lemon juice to brighten the flavor, along with some freshly chopped sorrel.

If you have room in your garden, sorrel is easy to grow and will provide you with an abundant supply of lemony leaves that can be used in salad as well as sauces. But you can also find it now in specialty grocers and farmers' markets.

Makes about 3 cups

Prep/cook time: 40 minutes

3 cups Fish Stock (page 28)
1 cup white wine
½ cup vermouth
3 to 4 shallots, minced
Salt and white pepper
Scant 1 cup heavy cream

Juice of 1 to 2 lemons
1 tablespoon Beurre Manié
  (page 35)
1 tablespoon Glace de Viande
  (page 25)
3 large bunches fresh sorrel

In a medium saucepan, combine the stock, wine, vermouth, and two-thirds of the shallots and bring to a boil. Reduce the heat and simmer until reduced by half, approximately 30 to 40 minutes. Add salt and pepper to taste. Strain into a bowl. Rinse the saucepan and pour the sauce back in.

Add the cream and the remaining shallots and bring to a boil. Reduce the heat and simmer until reduced by a third, approximately 15 to 20 minutes. Add juice from one lemon. Remove the pan from the heat and whisk in ½ tablespoon beurre manié. Return to the heat and allow to simmer for a few minutes. Add the glace de viande and continue simmering to incorporate. Taste and add additional lemon juice if necessary. If the mixture becomes too thick, dilute with a small amount of white wine; if it is too thin add the remaining beurre manié. Make sure the sauce is fully blended and taste for seasoning - add salt and white pepper.

While the sauce is cooking, wash, dry, and remove the center stems from the sorrel leaves, then cut in a rough julienne. You should have about 6 ounces or 3 to 4 cups of loosely packed sorrel.

Just before serving, add three-fourths of the sorrel leaves to the sauce and simmer until they "melt" into the sauce. Taste for acidity and add more lemon juice if necessary. If you are serving the sauce on top of salmon fillets, chiffonade the remaining sorrel leaves a bit more finely, scatter them on top of the sauced salmon, and serve immediately. If you are serving the sauce on the side, sprinkle the leaves on top of the sauce just before passing it at the table.

If you don't like the look of the sorrel leaves in the sauce, strain it just before serving and scatter the remaining fresh sorrel on top.

May 4, 196?

La Carte

Les Moules à la Poulette

Gigot d'Agneau
Provençal

Gratin Dauphinoise

Salade

Roulage Léontine

Café

Clos Blanc
de Vougeot
1962

Chateau
Latour 1952

VEGETABLES TO LOVE

Only two things money can't buy, that's true love and home grown tomatoes!

— Guy Clark, songwriter

How I got my kids to eat vegetables when I never did is a mystery. How Adrienne got me to love vegetables is a downright miracle. I can't think of a vegetable I really liked before I met Adrienne except fresh corn on the cob!

Adrienne grew a wide variety of vegetables and herbs in her garden on Long Island: cucumbers, squash, zucchini, eggplants of all shapes and colors, garlic, lettuces of every variety, and potatoes. But of all of them the best and most cared for were the tomatoes. Until I met Adrienne's tomato salad I was never really a fan of the tomato. Now I live for those late summer days when the tomato plants are groaning with ruby red beefsteaks.

TOMATE PROVENÇALE

Slow-Roasted Tomatoes and Garlic

This recipe comes from the restaurant Tetou in Golfe-Juan on the Côte d'Azure. The restaurant is literally on the beach, and you can be served with your toes stuck in the sand if you like. It is a place for simple, delicious seafood, most notably bouillabaisse. It is also a place for celebrities. The first time I was there, Sidney Poitier was sitting at the next table. Luckily the staff do not notice the difference between the famous, the infamous, and the rest of us; they treat everyone like family. The restaurant has been run by the Cirio family since the 1920s and most of the staff in the kitchen and dining room are family.

Adrienne often visited Tetou when she and her husband rented a house in Mougin for a month every spring. After about six years, they stopped renting regularly but whenever Adrienne got a yen for Tomate Provençale and bouillabaisse they would make a trip to the Cote d'Azure and Tetou.

Jacque Pierre, the grandson of the founder Ernest Cirio, shared with Adrienne the secret for making this intensely flavored roasted tomato dish, which is a perfect side to simply grilled fish or, of course, bouillabaisse. The intense tomato taste is the result of slowly roasting the tomatoes in a low oven. The tomatoes in the South of France do have a more intense flavor than the ones in the U.S., so we always include a bit of sun-dried tomato paste to make up for that. You can use any type of tomato for this recipe because it is the slow roasting that caramelizes the sugars in the tomatoes and gives them the rich flavor. The liquid that comes out during the cooking of the tomatoes has lots of flavor and should not be wasted. Store any leftovers in the freezer until you are making a sauce or vegetable dish that will benefit from an infusion of that tomato taste.

Serves 4 as a side

Prep time: ½ hour Total cook time: 2 hours 45 minutes

3 to 4 pounds tomatoes: plum, beefsteak, heirloom, etc.

5 cloves garlic, unpeeled

Salt and freshly ground black pepper

¼ cup chopped fresh basil

2 tablespoons chopped fresh oregano

2 tablespoons sun-dried tomato paste

1 clove garlic, finely chopped

1 cup fresh (not dried) bread crumbs*

2 tablespoons chopped fresh
    Italian flat-leaf parsley

Olive oil for drizzling

Preheat the oven to 250°F.

Lightly oil a rimmed baking sheet pan that will hold the tomatoes and any juice they will exude. Slice the tomatoes in half and crowd them into the pan cut side up. Tuck the unpeeled garlic cloves amongst them. Season with salt and pepper. Bake for 2 hours, until the tomatoes have shrunk in size and exuded quite a lot of liquid, which should be reserved. Let cool.

Increase the oven temperature to 450°F.

Pull the skins off the tomatoes and the garlic. If your tomatoes are not especially good they may have a tough woody center. Pull or cut this out but save all the juice that is exuded. This is a messy job, best done with your hands. The tomatoes will not look pretty but don't worry, it's the flavor that matters in this dish. Place the tomatoes in an oiled medium gratin dish with the cooked garlic (crushed a bit), the basil, oregano, salt, and pepper. Dot with the tomato paste and sprinkle the finely chopped garlic on the top. Add some of the tomato liquid that has seeped out while the tomatoes were cooling – but not too much, you don't want the tomatoes to be swimming in liquid. Some tomatoes tend to be more watery than others so save any excess liquid to use in another recipe. The dish can be held for several hours at this point.

Position the baking dish on the top rack in the oven and roast for 20 minutes. The sides of the tomatoes will caramelize a bit but don't let the rest burn. If they are cooking too fast, move to a lower position. Keep an eye out when roasting: If there is a lot of liquid in the dish pour it off and continue cooking.

Heat the broiler. Mix the fresh bread crumbs with the parsley and sprinkle on top of the tomatoes. Drizzle with olive oil. Broil 4 inches from the heat until the bread crumbs brown, about 5 minutes. Cool for 10 minutes and serve.

This dish would work well with any simply grilled fish or chicken.

---

* Fresh bread crumbs: Toss any stale bread, crusts removed, into a food processor and process until you have a fine crumb. If you don't have any stale bread, first dry out fresh sliced bread in a low oven for 15 to 20 minutes.

SIMCA BECK

In August and September, when the tomatoes are abundant, we gorge ourselves on the tomato salad recipe on page 56 because we know that the time for eating it at its best is finite. The salad epitomizes the best things of summer – the warmth of the sun, the sweet acidity of vine-ripened tomatoes, the crunch of sweet Vidalia onions, and the licorice taste of basil – all swimming in a perfectly balanced vinaigrette.

This simple recipe comes with a storied history. In 1965 Adrienne decided she wanted to take cooking lessons in France. Not knowing how to go about finding a teacher, she picked up the phone and called Craig Claiborne, the food critic for the New York Times *(whom she did not know at the time), to ask for a recommendation. He gave her Julia Child's number. Yes, that Julia Child. Unfortunately, Julia was living in the States at the time, but she recommended one of her co-authors on* Mastering the Art of French Cooking, *Simone (Simca) Beck. Simca had homes in Provence near Cannes and in Paris where she had a cooking school. She taught Adrienne the basics of French cooking and culture and they became good friends.*

One sunny afternoon Adrienne invited Simca to a poolside lunch at a house they were renting in Mougin, France. She served a fresh tomato salad as the first course. Simca proceeded to remove the skin from each slice of tomato with her knife and fork before she ate them. "The skins are not appealing and the tomato absorbs the vinaigrette better without them." She explained that the easiest way to remove the tomato skins before preparing the salad was to quickly blanch them in hot water and peel the skins away. To this day it is how we prepare the tomatoes for the salad.

Adrienne with Simca at Bramafam May 1971

SALADE D'ÉTÉ DE TOMATE

Summer Tomato Salad

In this recipe the measurements for the oil and vinegar are not given and what you end up with may not align with the classic 3:1 ratio for a vinaigrette. This is because the dressing will be influenced by the sweetness and acidity of the tomatoes. So each time you must taste, taste, taste to get the balance correct. You should use the best-quality vinegar and olive oil here because their taste will shine against the tomatoes.

Serves 4

Prep time: 45 minutes

6 to 8 large beefsteak or other meaty tomatoes

Good-quality balsamic vinegar

Extra virgin olive oil

1 Vidalia or other sweet onion, sliced very thin

Sea salt

Sherry vinegar

Freshly ground black pepper

2 large handfuls fresh basil leaves

1 large semolina baguette, sliced

2 (8-ounce) fresh buffalo mozzarella balls (not the rubbery ones), sliced

Bring a large pot of water to the boil. Half fill a large bowl with cold water. Make a small "X" in the skin of each tomato at the end opposite to the stem (where there is a small black dot or sometimes a series of irregular round black bumps). This will help the skin to peel off easily. Blanch 3 or 4 tomatoes in the boiling water for 3 to 5 minutes. You will see the skin crack and peel. Remove immediately and place in the cold water. Repeat with remaining tomatoes.

With a paring knife, peel the skin off the tomatoes and remove the stem and any white pith. Slice the tomatoes horizontally approximately ½ inch thick and layer them in a wide shallow serving bowl. Sprinkle each layer with balsamic and sherry vinegar, oil, some of the onion, and salt.

When you have all the tomatoes sliced, taste the liquid in the bowl for the oil/vinegar sweet/acid balance. Add more sherry vinegar and olive oil, as well as salt and pepper, as necessary. Unlike most salads, the dressing should pool in the bottom of the bowl. You should have about ½ cup of dressing in the bowl by the time you serve the salad. Taste again. If you are not sure about the balance, let the salad sit for 10 minutes to allow the juices of the tomatoes and the onions to blend with the oil and vinegar. Taste again for seasoning.

Chiffonade (chop or cut with scissors into fine strips) the basil and sprinkle on the salad just before serving. If you chop the basil before making the salad it will get discolored, so wait until just before serving. I find scissors are easier than a knife: Remove the leaves from each branch and stack them into piles. Fold the pile of leaves in half along the spine and, starting at the tip, scissor them into thin strips.

To Serve

Spoon some of the dressing from the bowl onto a slice of semolina bread, add a slice of buffalo mozzarella, then smother it with the tomatoes and more dressing and get ready for nirvana!

JEAN TROISGROS

In 1976 Jean Troisgros, three-star chef of Les Frères Troisgros in Roanne, France, stayed with Adrienne and her husband for a month at the house they rented in Mougin, a small town in the hills just above Cannes. Jean, along with his brother Pierre, led the group of chefs who developed the original nouvelle cuisine.

Jean was recovering from a kidney stone operation and did not have the stamina for shopping or cooking. Adrienne took full advantage of having a chef in residence. Each morning she went to the Marche Fourville in Cannes to buy the ingredients for dinner. Jean eagerly awaited her return and would often exclaim "Bien achete!" as she unpacked her purchases. They would then excitedly discuss the various possibilities for cooking what she had purchased.

At the end of his stay, Adrienne cooked dinner for friends and chefs who had come to visit Jean, among them Roger Vergé of Moulin de Mougin and Louis Outhier of L'Oasis. Including Jean, there were 11 Michelin stars at the table. A daunting task for anyone – unless you had been cooking with a three-star chef for a month! The menu included a baron of lamb and Gratin Dauphinoise.

As Adrienne was making the gratin, Jean exclaimed "Non, non, tu fait mal!" (No, you are doing it wrong!) She knew that she was not making the gratin in the traditional way Jean would have, so she ignored his admonitions. She had finagled the recipe from chef Raymond Thuilier of l'Oustau de Baumanière, whose gratin was so famous the restaurant gave the recipe to guests after their meal. But when Adrienne first made the recipe it did not turn out like the one served in the restaurant. She went back to Thuilier and told him that the recipe didn't work. With a wink and a nod he acknowledged that it was not quite accurate. He invited her into the kitchen and showed her how to do it correctly. This would happen repeatedly with "restaurant" recipes but Adrienne had no fear about asking for the real recipe! Just as she had no qualms about telling a three-star chef not to interfere with her gratin!

When the lamb was taken off the spit, Adrienne asked Roger to carve. As he did, he and Jean fell into a serious discussion. Adrienne was worried that she had overcooked the lamb, which would have been a disaster in front of all these chefs. Instead they told her the lamb had probably been lame when it was alive because they could tell the meat on one leg was quite inferior to the other! Adrienne was relieved that the fault wasn't in the cooking and they proceeded to carve only the uninjured leg, which was delicious.

During the meal Roger complimented Adrienne on the gratin (!) and asked for the recipe. She started to explain it to him, but Jean jumped up behind Roger's back and mouthed to her "Non, non, ne pas lui dire!" (No, don't tell him!) Jean didn't want Roger to have the recipe because of a prank Roger had played on him earlier in the evening, the details of which have been lost in time. In the end Adrienne shared the recipe with all the chefs.

Adrienne and Jean Troisgros at La Calade, Mougins 1974

GRATIN DAUPHINOISE D'ONZE ÉTOILE

Eleven-Star Potato Gratin

This is not a rich creamy gratin; it is almost a caramelized potato tart. The cream is reduced on the stove first, then the potatoes are added. The potatoes absorb the cream and cook in the remaining fat. Don't slice the potatoes in advance and hold them in water or you will have to dry them thoroughly before cooking.

Serves 8

Prep time: 30 minutes Cook time: 1½ hours

1 clove garlic, peeled

1 tablespoon unsalted butter

½ cup crème fraîche

1 cup heavy cream

4 large russet potatoes, peeled

4 large red bliss potatoes, peeled

Salt and freshly ground black pepper

1 teaspoon ground nutmeg

½ cup grated Parmesan cheese

Choose a ceramic-coated cast-iron casserole that you can use on the stove and in the oven. Cut the garlic clove in half and rub each half hard around the surface of the casserole. Smear the butter around the dish. Pour in the crème fraîche and ½ cup of cream. Place over medium-high heat and reduce – don't let it burn – until the mixture is very thick, like melted cheese. Remove from the heat.

Preheat the oven to 350°F.

Slice the potatoes on a mandolin very thin, as you would for chips. Layer them in the casserole with salt, pepper, and nutmeg. No more than three or four layers. Add the remainder of the cream to barely cover the potatoes. Press down on the potatoes to cover them with the cream. Return to medium heat and simmer until reduced slightly, 10 to 15 minutes. Again, don't let it burn.

Transfer the casserole to the oven and bake for 1 to 1¼ hours. The cream will have been absorbed by the potatoes and they will be brown and caramelized in the remaining fat. Add the grated Parmesan and return to the oven on the upper rack until the cheese has browned, about 15 minutes. Remove and allow to cool for 5 to 10 minutes.

My dear friend, Joanna, informs me that the addition of cheese means this is not a true gratin dauphinoise. She is right, but Adrienne called it a gratin dauphinoise and I am sticking to it!

POMMES ANNA

Potato Cake

A simple yet elegant dish that requires only potatoes, butter, goose fat, salt, and pepper! You will need a mandoline or food processor to slice the potatoes and a gratin dish or steel crepe pan that can be used on the stove and in the oven.

The potatoes begin cooking on the stove, frying in the fat as you arrange the slices in the pan. Then they go into the oven, covered, so they both steam and continue browning on the bottom and sides. What you end up with is a potato cake with a crunchy crust and a creamy center. It is best served immediately but if you must make it in advance remove it from the baking pan, wrap loosely in foil, and keep warm.

Serves 6 to 8

Prep/cook time: 1¼ hours

2 ½ to 3 pounds russet or Yukon gold potatoes, peeled

5 tablespoons unsalted butter, melted

¼ cup melted goose or duck fat, or vegetable oil

Salt and freshly ground black pepper

On a mandoline, or in food processor fitted with a slicing disk, slice the potatoes ⅛ to ¹⁄₁₆ inch thick. Place them immediately in a bowl and toss with the melted butter so they do not discolor. (Do not put them in water or you will have to dry them before cooking.)

Add the fat to a medium gratin dish or 9-inch crepe pan which can be used on the stove and in the oven. Place over medium-low heat and set a timer for 30 minutes. Begin to arrange the potato slices in the pan, starting in the center and fanning out in concentric circles. Sprinkle the first layer with salt and pepper. Continue layering the potatoes in circles and seasoning with salt and pepper until you have used all the slices. The layers should come almost up to the top of the pan. Continue cooking on the stove until the 30 minutes have elapsed. The heat should be low enough so the potatoes don't burn, but the fat should be bubbling. Press down on the top of the potatoes with a flat spatula to compress them while cooking. The bottom layer of potatoes and the edges will begin to brown.

Meanwhile, preheat the oven to 450°F.

When the timer is up, cover the pan with foil, pressing the foil right down on top of the potatoes to compact them and crimp around the sides. Transfer to the lower-middle oven rack and bake for 15 minutes. Uncover and continue baking for another 10 minutes, or until all the potatoes are soft, and the edges and what you can see of the underside are a nut brown color.

Drain off as much fat from the pan as possible by tilting it while holding the potatoes back with a spatula. Or, if you have a cake or pie pan you can hold the bottom against the potatoes and drain the fat into a container. Place a baking sheet on top of the pan and invert the potato cake onto the sheet. If any potatoes stick to the bottom scrape them up with a spatula and place them back on the cake. Transfer the cake to a warm serving plate and slice into wedges.

VEGETABLES AL FORNO

Baked Vegetables with Pesto

This wonderful dish makes use of all the abundant produce in the late summer. We always made double or triple the amount and froze it for use later. The original recipe appeared in *House & Garden* magazine in October 1976, but over the years Adrienne and I tweaked and experimented with the flavors and textures so now we consider it ours.

The proportions and ingredients are dependent on what is available in the market. It is important to peel both the tomatoes and peppers. Use a regular potato peeler. If you don't peel these vegetables, their skins come loose as they cook, which is unappealing in the finished dish. If you have made the caneton sauce on page 107, you will have some left-over herb mixture that you can use in this recipe to great effect. If not, make a pesto of the fresh herbs and oil as directed below.

Serves 5 to 6

Prep/cook time: 1 hour

1 cup chopped fresh thyme, marjoram, oregano, basil, and parsley; or ½ cup leftover herbs from making Caneton en Papillotte (page 107)

Olive oil

Salt and freshly ground black pepper

2 cups grated Parmesan cheese

3 medium red-skinned potatoes, sliced thin using a mandolin; or sliced ¼ inch thick and parboiled for 3 to 4 minutes

2 to 3 zucchini, sliced crosswise ¼ inch thick

3 to 4 tomatoes, peeled, seeded, and sliced ½ inch thick

1 medium eggplant, stemmed and sliced into long thin strips

2 bell peppers, peeled, seeded, and sliced ¼ inch thick

2 red onions, sliced as thin as possible

1 cup fresh bread crumbs (see page 57)

Preheat the oven to 375°F.

In a food processor, process the fresh herbs with 3 to 4 tablespoons olive oil, enough to make a loose paste.

In a large gratin dish (or foil pan(s) if you want to freeze all or part of the dish), arrange the potatoes on the bottom and sprinkle with salt and pepper. Top with about a tablespoon of the herb mixture, a third of a cup Parmesan, and a drizzle of olive oil. Continue layering each of the vegetables with the salt, pepper, herb mixture, Parmesan and oil in the order listed (zucchini, tomatoes, eggplant, peppers, onions). Top with bread crumbs and remaining Parmesan cheese. Bake for 40 to 45 minutes, until the vegetables are golden around the edges. Remove and serve. Alternatively, allow to cool, cover with foil and label before freezing.

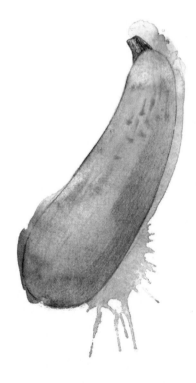

HARICOTS VERT AVEC MARJOLAINE ET CIBOULETTES

Green Beans with Marjoram and Shallots

A great Mediterranean side dish for any meal and a wonderful way to jazz up plain old green beans. This works best with thin beans, not the thicker, more robust green beans which require longer cooking. When Adrienne first made this, it was a revelation to me that green beans could be so interesting! The shallots provide a bit of crunch and the marjoram gives it the zing.

The beans are parboiled first and then finished with shallots, marjoram, and butter. The best way to check if they are done is to bite off a piece: If the bean is still a bit resistant but not crunchy then it is ready to be removed. The beans will cook a bit further after you cook the shallots but if they are still crunchy they will never cook enough, so err on the side of slightly overdone at first but try not to let them get too floppy.

Serves 4

Prep/cook time: 25 minutes

8 ounces thin green beans, trimmed	1 shallot, chopped medium fine
Salt	1 bunch marjoram, chopped – a good handful or about ⅓ cup
1 tablespoon unsalted butter	Freshly ground black pepper

Place the beans in saucepan and cover with boiling water. Add salt and simmer until the beans are al dente, about 10 minutes. Drain, rinse with cold water, and set aside.

In the same saucepan, melt the butter over medium heat. When the butter is foaming, add two-thirds of the shallots. Cook until translucent but not colored. Add the cooked beans and half the marjoram. Toss together and add salt and pepper – you will need a fair amount of both, particularly pepper, to get the right seasoning. Add the remaining shallot and cook for 3 to 5 minutes, until the beans are tender but not falling apart. Taste and correct seasoning. The dish can be held at this point.

Warm briefly before serving and add the remaining marjoram. The beans should taste strongly of the marjoram and pepper.

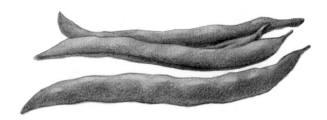

La Carte

Coquilles à la Nage
Puligny Montrachet 1969
Charmes - Henri Clerc
et Fils

Filet de Boeuf Périgourdine
Romanée St. Vivant 1961
Les Quatres Journaux
Louis Latour

Salade

Fromage

La Coupe

Thé   Café

FISH MADE EASY

Fish, to taste right, must swim three times – in water, in butter and in wine.

— Polish proverb

Before I met Adrienne, I never liked fish. I knew it was good for me and I ate it but I never liked it. After 25 years of cooking with Adrienne, I not only love fish but have grown fins and gills to prove it!

Many people are reluctant to cook fish, whether they like it or not, because they are worried about how to cook it. Fish is really no more difficult to cook than meat or chicken and usually takes less time. Determining when it is done is what usually puts people off. Adrienne was always actively touching the food she cooked. When you handle anything raw you begin to understand its texture. This helps you to know how the texture changes as it cooks so that you can tell when it is done to your liking by giving it a poke. Always wash your hands after handling raw fish or meat.

Start checking the fish after 6 to 8 minutes. Press the center of the fillet with your finger (or a spoon): if the fish gives way and flakes then it is fully cooked – which means overcooked! You want the center of the fillet to push back or be a bit bouncy rather than give way. When in doubt, take it out of the heat and pull apart the flakes in the center of the fillet. If it is translucent but not raw, and just comes away from the bone, it is not quite done. But take it off the heat, because it will continue cooking while it rests on the plate. A bit of practice will take the mystery out of judging when it is done.

Most of the recipes here feature fish that are very robust and difficult to overcook so don't be afraid. As with everything about cooking, if something goes wrong, "punt." Most classic recipes are the result of a kitchen mistake that was turned into an innovation. Overcooked fish can be turned into a delicious lunch salad with a bit of mayo, chopped parsley and chives served on a piece of toast. So dive in!

COQUILLES À LA NAGE

Scallops in Broth

This was the go-to first course for many of Adrienne's dinner parties. The recipe came from her time studying with Simca Beck and is a classic nouvelle cuisine dish. The ingredients are lightly cooked to preserve their fresh taste and the broth is a reduction of fish stock and wine with just a bit of crème fraîche to give it body. The delicate taste of the scallops and the vegetables remain the highlight. It is the perfect dish for a dinner party because you can make most of it in advance. The amounts here are for a first course, but you can easily serve it as a main course for four by increasing the scallops to 2 pounds in total.

Serves 6 as a first course

Prep/cook time: 1½ hours

3 tablespoons unsalted butter

½ pound white or brown button mushrooms, stemmed and sliced ¼ inch thick

4 ½ ounces fine julienne (cut like matchsticks) of carrots (don't include the woody centers)

4 ½ ounces finely sliced leeks, white parts only

½ pound snow pea pods (not sugar snap peas)

4 cups Fish Stock (page 27)

⅔ cup white wine

⅔ cup crème fraiche

1½ pounds sea scallops, muscle removed* and sliced into discs about ⅜ inch thick

Freshly squeezed lemon juice

Salt and freshly ground black pepper

In a sauté pan, melt 2 tablespoons of the butter over medium-high heat until foaming. Add the mushrooms and cook until they render some juice but are still firm, about 5 minutes. With a slotted spoon, transfer the mushrooms to a bowl.

Add the remaining 1 tablespoon butter to the pan with the mushroom liquid. When it has melted, add the carrots and simmer for 5 minutes. Add the leeks and cook for an additional 10 minutes, until they are wilted and translucent; don't let the vegetables color. Remove from the heat.

Meanwhile, parboil the snow peas in a saucepan of boiling water with a good teaspoon of salt just until al dente, about 7 minutes. Drain and refresh with cold water to stop the cooking. Trim off the side without the peas (creating two narrow pods). Keep warm.

In a saucepan, combine one-third of the carrot and leek mixture with all the fish stock and white wine; boil until reduced by a third. Reduce the heat to low and add the scallops. Never allowing the liquid to even simmer, poach the scallops until just opaque and slightly firm to the touch, 5 to 10 minutes. Recall how the scallops felt when you put them into the liquid, kind of squidgy. They should now feel a bit firmer, still not quite cooked through but definitely not raw. They will continue to cook when you add the hot broth later in the recipe. Remove the scallops to a dish and keep warm. Strain out the vegetables and return the liquid to the saucepan.

Whisk the crème fraîche into the fish stock liquid. Boil quite hard until reduced by half. Taste for seasoning and add salt, pepper, and lemon juice. You should have a light, clean, fish taste with a bit of lemony brightness. Reduce heat to simmering point. *You can turn off the heat at this point and hold the dish for about an hour. When you reheat the liquid bring it back to a boil and then reduce to a simmer before continuing with the recipe.*

Add the rest of the carrot/leek mixture and mushrooms to the fish stock liquid and gently heat to just barely simmering. Add any juice that has leached out of the scallops as they have been resting. Taste again for seasoning. Gently reheat the peapods in a saucepan with a little butter (if you made the recipe in advance, add the scallops in with the peapods to bring them up to temperature).

Using warmed dishes that are slightly concave (a shallow soup bowl is ideal) place a few pea pods on the bottom, spoon the scallops on top, then the broth and vegetables and finally place more pea pods on top.

---

*Scallops are often sold with the remnant of the muscle that attaches it to the shell. This rough strip along the side of the scallop about ¾ inch long should be removed using your fingers or a knife.

COQUILLES AVEC SABAYON AU RIESLING

Scallops with Riesling Sabayon

This easy yet elegant sauce comes from Pierre Wynants, the former chef of Comme chez Soi restaurant in Brussels. The name of the restaurant translates as "Like at Home," meaning that the chef is cooking for you as if you were in his home.

Everything that came out of Pierre's kitchen was simply wonderful, but this sauce is sublime. It is an unsweetened sabayon – another emulsion – and must be served immediately. It has four ingredients and takes very little time to prepare, but it will astound you with its sophisticated taste. Adrienne served it on simply sautéed scallops with new potatoes and thin beans for a *Comme chez Soi* meal.

Serves 4

Prep/cook time: 30 minutes

1 to 2 tablespoons unsalted butter

12 to 16 medium to large scallops, muscle* removed

2 egg yolks

¼ cup Riesling or other similar white wine

1 to 2 teaspoons fresh squeezed lemon juice

2 teaspoons clarified unsalted butter**

Scallops

Select a sauté pan large enough to accommodate all the scallops without crowding. If necessary, use two pans. Place over medium-high heat, add the butter, and cook until foaming. Add the scallops and cook for 3 to 5 minutes, just until lightly browned, then turn and cook for another 3 minutes. If in doubt about the cooking time, remove one scallop and slice in half – it should be translucent in the center but not raw. Remove the scallops to a warm plate and cover with foil.

Sauce

In a copper or heavy-bottomed, pan, whisk together the egg yolk and wine. Place over very low heat and cook and continue whisking while you increase the heat slowly to medium high. The mixture will begin to foam and then swell into a light, soft mass. It is done when it forms soft mounds at the end of the whisk, which will take 5 to 7 minutes. Whisk in 1 tablespoon lemon juice and the clarified butter and taste for acidity; add the remaining lemon juice as needed Season with salt and pepper.

Place the scallops on warmed plates and dress with the sauce.

---

* Scallops are often sold with the remnant of the muscle that attaches it to the shell. This rough strip along the side of the scallop about ¾ inch long should be removed with your fingers or a knife.

** To clarify butter, melt 2 teaspoons butter in the microwave; measure out 1 teaspoon of the clear yellow liquid; discard the solids at the bottom.

PIERRE WYNANTS
Comme chez Soi Restaurant

Pierre Wynants inscribed these words to Adrienne in his cookbook, Creative
Belgian Cuisine:

> *For indulgent pleasure and happiness, there is nothing like a
> flavor from the heart.*

> *And my most delicious friendship is with Martin and Adrienne.*

ALAIN CHAPEL
Chez La Mère Charles

In 1971 André Soltner, then the chef at Lutèce in NYC, competed for and won the Meilleur Ouvrier de France, the first non-resident Frenchman to win for cooking. Competing with him was Alain Chapel, chef of the then two-star (soon to be three -star) Chez La Mère Charles restaurant in Mionnay outside Lyon. André was impressed with Alain's cuisine and expertise in the kitchen. Upon his return to NYC he urged Adrienne to visit M. Chapel's restaurant. On the next trip to France a detour to Mionnay was made with a reservation mentioning the recommendation from the new Meilleur Ouvrier.

They were the first Americans to arrive at the restaurant and M. Chapel insisted on making a menu for them, including his famous Gateau de Foie Blond. Below are Adrienne's notes from the meal and her ratings for each dish. See page 87 for more details about her rating system.

__Omble Chevalier beurre fondu caviar hollandaise__ – a lovely delicate omble (char) about the size of a large trout, skinned and boned at the table directly from the poacher it was cooked in; exquisite with the beurre fondu and hollandaise mixed together. (18)

__Gateau de foie blond sauce écrevisse Lucien Tendret__ – incredible almost indescribable airy hot liver "mousse" with a rich but delicate écrevisse sauce with one whole large écrevisse as garnish. (20)

__Ortolans__ – 2 each – exquisite and simple. (17)

__Becassine__ – one for 2 – __and a Grieve__ one each, done en cocotte; the Becassine (Snipe) was new to us and I thought it very juicy and exciting, the Grieve was good but we're not wild about it; served with little crepes of pommes pailles, truffles and parsley and crisp, delicious creamed champignons de bois. (17)

__Fromage Blanc__ with crème fraiche served from the metal farm container it was sold in – absolutely fantastic slightly acid combination of half cow/half goat's milk . (19)

Then a mélange of ice cream for dessert – all excellent. (17)

__Wine__: Pouilly Fuisse 1969 and Moulin à Vent

After dinner I questioned M. Chapel about the use of the word "Gateau" for the foie blond dish. Evidently it's a traditional term used because the dish is made like a flan and a flan is usually a dessert.

Adrienne and Alain Chapel 1974. A food friendship was born!

SAUMON EN PAPILLOTTE AVEC BEURRE ROUGE

Salmon with Red Wine Butter Sauce

Adrienne first encountered salmon in red wine sauce at Comme chez Soi in Brussels. It was unusual and divine, like so many of Pierre Wynants's dishes. But her notes for this sauce are based on one that Alain Chapel served while he was a guest chef at the Four Seasons Hotel in New York in 1977. She re-created it to inspire her husband to take a really good bottle of red out of the cellar.

This sauce is not as delicate an emulsion as the classic beurre blanc. In addition, you can refrigerate it for several days and reheat it gently over low heat. Don't microwave it or it will separate. It will keep in the freezer for up to a year. Add a few boiled new potatoes or polenta and the haricots vert on page 66 for a three-star meal! This method for cooking the salmon lends itself to a variety of other sauces, such as the sorrel sauce on page 48.

Serves 4

Prep/cook time: sauce, 1 hour; fish, 20 minutes

Beurre Rouge

10 tablespoons (1¼ sticks) cold
    unsalted butter

2 small carrots, finely diced

½ cup finely diced onion

¼ cup finely diced celery

Sprig fresh thyme

1 bay leaf

Pinch salt

1½ cups Fish Stock (page 27)

1 tablespoon red wine vinegar,
    plus more if needed

2 cups red wine

Salmon

4 salmon fillets, 4 to 6 ounces
    each

4 tablespoons olive oil

4 sprigs fresh thyme

Salt and freshly
    ground black
    pepper

Beurre Rouge

In a saucepan, melt 2 tablespoons of the butter over medium heat. Add the carrots, onion, celery, thyme, bay leaf, and salt and sauté until barely softened. Add the stock and vinegar and simmer until reduced by half; about 15 minutes. Add the red wine and reduce by half; about 30 minutes. Strain to remove the vegetables and return the liquid to pan.

Cut the remaining 8 tablespoons butter into 8 pieces. Whisk the butter into the sauce, one piece at a time, until it is creamed into the sauce. Taste and correct for seasoning – salt, pepper, additional vinegar. Keep warm over very low heat.

Salmon

Preheat the oven to 350°F.

Place each salmon fillet on a piece of foil large enough to enclose it. Sprinkle with 1 tablespoon olive oil, a sprig of thyme, and salt and pepper. Bring the long edges of the foil to meet and crimp or fold them over so the foil fits snugly around the fillet, then crimp or fold the short ends. Place in a shallow baking dish that will hold all four packages. Bake for 10 to 15 minutes, depending on the thickness of the fillets. Carefully unwrap one foil package to check for doneness: Using a spoon or your fingers press on the fillet - if it begins to flake or separate and the center is rare, they are done. If the fillet is very bouncy and doesn't flake or separate, return the packets to the oven for 3 to 5 minutes. Remove from oven and allow to sit in the foil for 3 to 5 minutes to finish cooking.

Place a small pool of sauce about 2 inches in diameter on each warm plate; remove the skin and place the salmon fillets on top; spoon additional sauce down the length of the fillet and serve.

SOLE À LA CRÈME DE ROMARIN

Sole with Rosemary Sauce

Adrienne loved pairing unusual ingredients, such as this rosemary-cream sauce from the master saucier Frédy Girardet with Dover sole or gray sole – sublime! You can also use it on sea bass, as Frédy did in February 1982, for an invitation-only dinner at Le Cirque in New York City. It was one of the few times Frédy left his restaurant in Crissier, Switzerland. Due to the strong rosemary taste, it does not translate well to all fish – as Adrienne discovered when she was having an impromptu dinner party and couldn't find sole or sea bass. She substituted striped bass and found the taste of the sauce fought with the fish. She made a quick sauce vierge instead and saved the rosemary sauce for another day.

Serves 4 as a main; 8 as a first course

Prep/cook time: 40 minutes

2½ pints cream

6 branches fresh rosemary

1 pint crème fraîche

1 cup Fish Stock (page 27)

½ cup white wine

Salt and freshly ground black pepper

1 lemon, halved

8 Dover or grey sole fillets, 4 ounces each

Preheat the oven to 350°F.

Combine the cream and four branches of rosemary in a saucepan and boil until reduced to about ¼ cup. Stir occasionally and do not let the cream burn. The cream will have a very concentrated, almost medicinal taste of rosemary. Remove the rosemary branches and any loose needles.

Pour the concentrated cream into a clean saucepan and add the crème fraîche, stock, white wine, salt and pepper. Simmer gently. Taste for seasoning. Squeeze in some lemon juice, a few teaspoons at a time, tasting between each addition, until you have a nice acidity that is not overwhelming. Keep the sauce warm while you prepare the fish.

Film a baking dish with a small amount of stock so the fillets don't stick. Place the fillets in a single layer in the pan and bake for 7 to 8 minutes, until cooked through. Test a fillet by pressing with your finger or a spoon: If it gives way but the flesh is still translucent, it is done. The cooking time will be a bit more for Dover sole, 10 to 12 minutes.

Reheat the sauce to almost boiling with a few branches of fresh rosemary. If serving as a main course, place two cooked fillets on each of four warmed plates or shallow bowls. For a first course serve one fillet per person. Remove the rosemary branches from the sauce and serve the sauce on top of the fillets. Serve with steamed potatoes or rice.

LA GRIBLETTE DE BAR AU JUS D'OIGNON ROSE ET FUMET DE CHOU VERT

Sea Bass with Red Onion Jus and Green Cabbage

This dish, from the *cuisine minceur* (literally "slimming cooking") inventor Michel Guérard, is an unusual combination of cabbage, red onions, and sea bass fillets that creates a perfect fusion of taste. The name itself is a bit of a pun which reveals Michel's mischievous sense of humor. A *griblette* is a larded piece of meat which you would normally serve with cabbage and a jus. Michel has turned that traditional concept inside out by using fish rather than meat and jus from onions.

We first had this dish at his Les prés d'Eugénie restaurant in Eugénie-les-Bain in 2006 and were stunned by the combination of taste and texture. Adrienne and Michel discussed the method of cooking the various ingredients at great length during our meal. The next day he presented her with the recipe opposite, written in his own hand.

The sauce can be made a day in advance, and the fried onions can be done an hour or more ahead and kept warm. Do not discard the sautéed onions used to make the jus. Tuck them into the fridge until you have time to check out the recipe for Pissaladiere Niçoise in *Mastering the Art of French Cooking.*

Michel Guérard

Les prés d'Eugénie

La Griblette de Bar au Jus d'Oignon Rosé

INGRÉDIENTS POUR 4 PERSONNES :

4 GRIBLETTES DE BAR DE 120g (ESCALOPES TAILLÉES EN BIAIS UN PEU ÉPAISSES) *peu épaisses*

4 OIGNONS ROUGES MOYENS

5g DE VINAIGRE DE VIN

20g DE BEURRE DEMI SEL

CHOU VERT FRISÉ OU CHOUX DE BRUXELLES (AU CHOIX SELON LES POSSIBILITÉS)

Pour la Sauce :

3 OIGNONS ROUGES

UN PEU DE THYM

15g DE BEURRE

30g DE VINAIGRE DE VIN

½ l D'EAU

70g DE BEURRE MONTÉ

Progression de la recette

la Sauce :

- EMINCER 3 OIGNONS ROUGES ET LES FAIRE REVENIR AVEC LE THYM DANS LES 15g DE BEURRE.

- DÉGLACER AVEC LES 30g DE VINAIGRE DE VIN

- RÉDUIRE PRESQUE À SEC ET MOUILLER AVEC LE ½ L. D'EAU

- CUIRE DOUCEMENT PENDANT 1 HEURE, PASSER AU CHINOIS, RÉDUIRE À NOUVEAU JUSQU'À OBTENIR 100g DE JUS D'OIGNON

- AJOUTER ALORS LES 70g DE BEURRE MONTÉ. RECTIFIER L'ASSAISONNEMENT

- MAINTENIR AU CHAUD.

- EMINCER LES 4 OIGNONS ROSES, LES FAIRE SUER AVEC LES 20g DE BEURRE DEMI SEL

- LES AMENER À LA CUISSON LÉGÈREMENT CROQUANTE

- CISELER LES FEUILLES DE CHOU FRISÉ, LES BLANCHIR À L'EAU BOUILLANTE SALÉE.

- S'IL S'AGIT DES CHOUX DE BRUXELLES, BLANCHIR 1 SECONDE LES BELLES FEUILLES ET CISELER LE CŒUR ET SUER À L'HUILE D'OLIVE.

- MÉLANGER LE CHOU CHOISI AUX OIGNONS.

- CUIRE LE BAR AU FOUR À 150° EN LE BADIGEONNANT D'HUILE D'OLIVE (IL EST CUIT À 47° À CŒUR)

DRESSAGE :

- DISPOSER AU FOND D'UNE ASSIETTE CREUSE LES OIGNONS ET LES FEUILLES DE CHOU CISELÉ

- POSER DESSUS LES GRIBLETTES DE BAR

- DÉCORER AVEC QUELQUES FEUILLES DE CHOU DE BRUXELLES, PLUCHES DE CERFEUIL, FLEUR DE SEL ET POIVRE MIGNONETTE AUXQUELLES ON AJOUTE QUELQUES ROUELLES D'ÉCHALOTE LÉGÈREMENT FARINÉES ET FRITES DANS LE BEURRE CLARIFIÉ.

- ÉMULSIONNER LA SAUCE AU MIXER AVANT DE LA VERSER AUTOUR DES GRIBLETTES.

BON APPÉTIT !

Michel

Serves 4

Prep/cook time: sauce 1½ hours; fish and cabbage 45 minutes

Sauce

6 tablespoons (¾ stick) unsalted butter, at room temperature

3 red onions, sliced ¼ inch thick

Sprig of fresh thyme

2 tablespoons white wine vinegar

2 cups water

Salt and freshly ground black pepper

Champagne vinegar or Banyuls vinegar

Melt 2 tablespoons of butter in a sauté pan over medium-high heat. When it foams, add the onions and thyme; sauté for about 5 minutes, until onions are tender and translucent. Don't let them brown. Deglaze the pan with white wine vinegar and reduce until almost dry, about 10 minutes. Add the water and cook over low heat for 1 hour, until the onions are soft and sweet tasting. Strain through a sieve, reserving liquid. Refrigerate onions for another use. Return onion liquid to the pan and reduce again to about ½ cup. Add the remaining 4 tablespoons butter and boil vigorously for 2 to 3 minutes. Season with salt, pepper and a dash of Champagne vinegar as needed. Keep the sauce warm; *or,* if making ahead, pour into a container and refrigerate. Bring to room temperature before reheating.

Fish, Onions, and Cabbage

1 to 2 tablespoons unsalted butter

4 medium red onions, sliced ¼ inch thick

1 small savoy cabbage, core removed and leaves cut in ½-inch strips

4 fillets of sea bass, 4 to 5 ounces each

Olive oil for brushing

Fresh chervil or parsley sprigs

Coarse salt and freshly ground black pepper

Preheat the oven to 350°F. Melt 1 tablespoon butter in a sauté pan over high heat. When it foams, add onions and reduce heat to medium. Sweat the onions (cook slowly without browning) for 2 to 3 minutes. Increase the heat to high and cook until slightly crunchy but not burned, about 10 minutes. Add an additional tablespoon of butter if necessary. Drain on a paper towel and keep warm until ready to serve.

Bring a pot of salted water to boil. Add cabbage and cook until just tender, 5 to 10 minutes. The only way to tell if it is cooked is to bite a piece: It should have a bit of resistance, but not hard. Drain and return to the pan. Briefly toss to dry over medium heat. Remove from heat but keep warm.

While the cabbage is cooking, make three diagonal slashes on each sea bass fillet through the skin, just into the flesh. Brush the fillets with olive oil. Place them skin side up in a baking pan; place on the top rack in the oven. Bake until the skin crisps and the flesh is cooked through, 10 to 15 minutes. If the skin starts to burn, move the pan down to the middle rack.

Presentation

Divide most of the fried onions and the cabbage among four slightly concave plates. Top with the sea bass. Decorate with the remaining cabbage, fried onions and sprigs of chervil or parsley. Season with coarse salt and ground pepper and dress with the warmed sauce.

FLETÁN PROVENÇAL AVEC PIMENT ET FENOUIL

Provençal Halibut with Peppers and Fennel

This is Adrienne's version of a quickie bouillabaisse. You will need very good fish stock to start and a nice thick piece of halibut. Hake also works very well in this dish and is less expensive. In no more than an hour you will have a hearty fish soup with a bit of a kick to it. Serve with a hot baguette and spicy provençal rouille if you have it, or butter if you don't.

Serves 4

Prep/cook time: 1 hour

Soup

2 cups Fish Stock (page 27)

Pinch of saffron

Top of 1 fennel bulb with fronds; or ¼ teaspoon fennel seeds, crushed

½ cup crab or lobster broth from the fishmonger, or Shellfish Stock (page 29)

1 cup white wine

½ cup Court Bouillon (page 30), optional

Vegetables

1 tablespoon olive oil

1 fennel bulb, quartered, cored, and sliced into ¼-inch strips

1 red bell pepper, peeled, seeded, and sliced into ¼-inch strips

1 tablespoon Knorr Tamarind Soup Mix*

10 small baby white or creamer potatoes, cut into quarters; or 4 to 5 Yukon Gold potatoes peeled, halved, and sliced ½ inch thick

Soup

Combine the fish stock, saffron, fennel top or seeds, crab/lobster broth, wine, and court bouillon (if using) in a saucepan and boil until reduced by half. Strain and set aside

Vegetables

Heat the olive oil in a sauté pan over medium heat. Add the sliced fennel and bell pepper and cook until soft but not browned, about 15 minutes. Set aside.

While the fennel and peppers are cooking, add the tamarind soup mix to 1 quart water and bring to a simmer to dissolve the soup mix. Add the potatoes and cook until tender, about 15 minutes. Drain, reserving the liquid, and keep the potatoes warm.

Fish

1 pound halibut or hake, 1 inch thick, skin removed
About ¾ cup white wine
About 2 tablespoons white wine vinegar
About 2 tablespoons Court Bouillon (page 31) or water
½ pound shrimp, peeled and deveined, optional

Preheat the oven to 350°F.

Place the halibut in a fish poacher or other deep casserole. Fill the pan not quite halfway up the side of the fish with a combination of the wine, vinegar, and court bouillon. You may need more than the amounts indicated of combined wine/vinegar/bouillon, depending on the size of the pan and the thickness of the fish. Cover the pan, transfer to the oven, and bake for 7 minutes.

If using shrimp, add them to the halibut. Bake for another 3 to 5 minutes. The halibut should still be slightly undercooked, but not raw, as it will continue cooking in the hot soup. Remove the halibut and shrimp from the broth, cover them with foil, and keep warm. Do not discard cooking liquid.

continued

Finishing

Hot sauce, cayenne pepper, or
powdered rouille

6 tablespoons (¾ stick) unsalted
butter, at room temperature,
cut into pieces

12 fresh basil leaves

Bring the fish soup to a boil. Add a generous dash of hot sauce (or pepper or rouille), a tablespoon or two of the reserved potato cooking liquid, and 1 to 2 tablespoons of the fish cooking liquid. Taste, adding more of the potato or fish liquid if necessary for thickening and flavor. Lower the heat to a simmer and beat in the butter by tablespoons. Taste and correct for seasoning. It should have a bit of a kick to it but still have a great rich fish taste.

Divide the potatoes, fennel, and peppers between two bowls and lay the halibut and shrimp over the vegetables. Ladle the very hot fish broth over the top. Julienne the basil leaves and sprinkle on top. Serve with chunks of warm baguette smeared with rouille or butter.

Adrienne discovered Knorr Tamarind Soup Mix in a tiny specialty food store on Rue Maître Albert near the Maubert-Mutualite metro station in Paris. She bought the packages for no particular reason, but when she got back home and tasted the broth, which has a lovely lemony taste, she found endless uses for it. It is a staple in Asian cooking, particularly with shellfish. We always stocked up on it whenever we were in Paris. Now of course you can buy it online.

Halibut is called "Heaven Fish" in its native waters of Norway.

STAR RATINGS

By the time I met Adrienne she and her husband had been travelling and compiling notes on every meal for 25 years. In the very beginning they rated the dishes "great" or "fabulous" or even "Not Good." Then they started using the one-star, two-star and three-star system for consistency and comparison. But even that didn't allow for enough nuanced detail between a two star that was almost a three star or a three star that was off the charts. So they developed their own system that assigned a range to each star rating. This helped them keep track of the quality of the meals and determine if they should continue frequenting a restaurant and if they should even order the same dish again. Anal? You bet! Here is how it worked:

> *3*** equals 17 to 19*
>
> > *20 is beyond 3*** it was rare and ethereal*
>
> *2** equals 14 to 16*
>
> *1* equals 11 to 13*
>
> > *10 is nothing special*
> >
> > *Below 10 meant the chef should be caned!*

For a dish to be a 20 it had to be perfectly conceived, with nothing extraneous on the plate, and unique. A steak, no matter how delicious and perfectly cooked, would never be a 20. But Michel Guérard's La Griblette de Bar au Jus d 'Oignon Rose et Fumet de Chou Vert (see page 80) was a 20 when we first had it in May 2006 and again in April 2007. Furthermore, if you had a dish that was a 16 in a two-star restaurant that would be very good. But a dish rated a 16 in a three-star restaurant meant that the chef had stumbled.

After a few years of traveling and eating with Adrienne, she began to include my ratings in her notes…I felt like I'd been promoted to Sous Chef!

FRUTTI DI MARE CON PESTO LINGUINE

Shellfish with Pesto Pasta

Adrienne was never good at judging how much to plant in her garden on Long Island; she always planted too much. Each winter as she pored over the seed and plant catalogues, her husband would remind her that she had promised to cut back on the amount she planted. Thank goodness she never listened to him when it came to basil. She was passionate about basil. She planted an entire raised bed devoted to basil: giant leaved varieties, Italian specialties, small leaved cinnamon Thai basil, lemon basil, purple basil (because it looked so pretty), and many others that I have forgotten. Which meant of course that we made pesto...Did we make pesto!

You can freeze pesto if you too have an over abundance of basil. Then you can use it all year to dress a fillet of fish or chicken, or spice up a sauce vierge. The basil taste will fade a bit the longer it is kept frozen, but in the dead of winter that pesto will taste like summer sunshine on pasta. When you store the pesto, in the freezer or the fridge, film the top of the container with olive oil so that the basil doesn't turn black. If you freeze the pesto add the Parmesan only when it is thawed. It should keep in the fridge for a week in an airtight container. In the freezer, it should last the winter.

The scallops and shrimp makes pasta with pesto a bit more festive and requires very little effort. If you have the pesto in the freezer this can be an easy weekday meal. Serve a green salad after the pasta on the same plate – the way they do in country restaurants in Italy – to sop up the remaining sauce. A nice piece of gorgonzola cheese would be the perfect end to the meal.

Serves 6 to 8

Prep/cook time: pesto 30 minutes; shellfish and pasta 45 minutes

Pesto

3 cups packed fresh basil leaves, about 3 bunches

1 clove garlic, peeled

¼ cup pine nuts (pignoli)

About ½ cup extra virgin olive oil

½ cup grated Parmesan cheese (omit if freezing the pesto)

Salt

Shellfish

4 tablespoons unsalted butter

2 pounds shrimp, shelled and deveined

2 pounds scallops, muscle* removed

Pasta

1½ boxes (24 ounces total) good-quality linguine

Salt

Freshly grated Parmesan

Pesto

Remove the leaves from the basil branches. If the leaves are very large, remove the thick vein in the center. Wash if necessary and pat dry. Put the basil leaves, garlic clove, pine nuts, ¼ cup of the oil, the Parmesan (if using), and a good pinch of salt in a food processor. Blend, stopping to scrape down the sides, until puréed, 2 to 3 minutes. It should be thick but not a paste. If it is too thick, add a bit more oil. If too thin, add more cheese and basil. Taste and correct seasoning – add more garlic or Parmesan to your taste. Pour into a container and film the top with a bit of olive oil.

Shellfish

In a sauté pan, melt the butter over medium-high heat until foaming. Add the shrimp and sauté just until they turn pink. Remove from pan. Add the scallops and cook, turning once, until just browning on the edges and still a bit translucent in the center (they will continue to cook further in the sauce). Remove the scallops and cut in half or quarters if large. Keep warm.

Pasta

Meanwhile, bring a large pot of salted water to boil. Add the linguine and cook until al dente. Drain the pasta, saving ½ cup of the cooking liquid. Return the linguine to the pot and add the shellfish, 3 to 4 tablespoons pesto, and ¼ cup of the pasta water. Cook over low heat, tossing to combine. Taste for seasoning and add additional tablespoons of pesto until you have the right taste and texture. Add additional pasta water if the mixture becomes too thick. Serve immediately garnished with the grated Parmesan.

---

* *Scallops are often sold with the remnant of the muscle that attaches it to the shell. This rough strip along the side of the scallop about ¾ inch long should be removed with your fingers or a knife.*

HOMARD PRINCE VLADIMIR

Lobster in Champagne Sauce

This dish was created in Illhaeusern at the lovely Auberge de l'Ill by three-star chef Paul Haeberlin over 50 years ago, and it is showing no signs of age. I first tasted it in 1993 at Adrienne's insistence and was seduced by the delicate sauce – which in no way overwhelms the sweet taste of the lobster. And this from a girl who grew up eating lobsters on Cape Cod. How it came to be called "Prince Vladimir" is anyone's guess – I think it was a bit of clever marketing on the part of the chef.

The key to making the dish, aside from great lobster, is the stock which is made from the lobster shells. Now the problem is that you probably do not have a freezer full of lobster shells unless you live on the New England coast. So the alternative is lobster or shellfish broth from the fish market. Don't use lobster bisque or soup as that will be too rich. Of course, once you have made this dish you will have the lobster shells and you can make yourself some lovely homemade stock!

Raw lobster meat is like jelly so the lobsters must be blanched first in order to remove the meat from the tail and claws. You will need kitchen shears or lobster shears to get the meat out of the tail and claws and a spoon to remove the green tomalley from the body. If you aren't too sure about handling and cooking lobsters, I encourage you to search for Julia Child's "The Lobster Show" on YouTube. It is a classic and you will learn everything there is to know about lobsters!

Serves 4

Prep/cook time: 1½ hours

Lobster Stock

2 cups lobster or shellfish broth from a fishmonger, or Shellfish Stock (page 29)

2 cups Court Bouillon (page 30)

1 tablespoon chopped fresh tarragon

Lobsters and Sauce

4 live lobsters, 1½ pounds each

2 cups dry Champagne

4 tablespoons unsalted butter, softened

½ cup crème fraîche

Freshly squeezed lemon juice

Salt and freshly ground black pepper

1 teaspoon beurre manié (see
  page 35), optional

1 teaspoon chopped fresh
  tarragon

Lobster Stock

Combine the lobster broth, court bouillon, and tarragon in a saucepan, bring to a simmer, and simmer until reduce by half, about 20 minutes. Set aside.

Lobsters

While the stock is simmering, bring a pot of water that will hold the lobsters to a boil. Plunge the lobsters headfirst into the pot, cover, and cook for 1 minute. Remove the lobsters to a drain board. Remove the claws and tail with a pair of scissors. Remove the green tomalley (liver) from the body, reserving two. Discard the rest of the innards from the body of the lobsters but reserve the shells and spiny legs for making stock at a later date. You can freeze them, along with the tail and claw shells once you remove the meat.

Crack the claws and split the underside of the tail with the scissors from the top to the bottom to remove the meat. Reserve as much of the milky liquid that comes out of the lobster as possible.

Preheat the oven 350°F.

Place the claw and tail meat in a casserole that can go on the stove and in the oven. Add the Champagne and lobster stock; bring to a simmer. Transfer the skillet to the oven and bake for 5 minutes.

Sauce

Force the tomalley and butter through a sieve into a bowl. Whisk in the crème fraîche. Remove the lobster from the oven, the meat should be firm, still slightly opaque but not raw. Remove the meat to a warm plate. Strain the liquid into a saucepan and reduce over high heat to approximately 2 cups. Beat ½ cup of this sauce into the tomalley mixture in a steady stream. Then add the mixture back into the saucepan. Add a squeeze of lemon juice, 1 to 2 tablespoons of the lobster liquid, salt and pepper to taste. You should have a light textured sauce with a concentrated lobster taste. If you want to thicken the sauce, add a teaspoon of beurre manié and simmer for an additional 10 minutes.

Briefly add the lobster meat to the saucepan then serve immediately in warmed bowls garnished with the tarragon.

La Carte

Croustade de Poisson

Beurre Blanc

Clos Blanc de Vougeot
1962

Pigeonneaux aux Morilles

Bonnes Mares - Belongey
1945

Salade

Fromage   Port - Hoopers 1931

Crème d'ananas

NOT JUST CHICKEN

Always start out with a larger pot than you think you need.

— Julia Child

There is nothing not to like about chicken but Adrienne was fond of all our feathered friends and the different ways of bringing out their flavors. Some of the recipes here are old-fashioned braises like Rosemary Lemon Chicken and Potatoes, but others will surprise you with their unique flavors. Try the Sweet and Sour Chicken from Jean Troisgros and you will never again say chicken is boring. Don't let the more complex recipes put you off. The Pigeonneaux aux Morilles recipe looks daunting but most of it can be done in advance. Give it a go! The first time I made it Adrienne and I had not yet started cooking together. My old friend, and fellow foodie, Kathryn was visiting from California and I wanted to make a special meal for her. Adrienne gave me the recipe and talked me through the concept and off I went! It wasn't just special, it was an historic meal! Encouraged by that success, I enticed the same friend back a few years later for Caneton en Papillotte. Another win!

Cooking has often been described as learning from your mistakes, which we all do. But we also learn confidence from our successes. After making the Pigeonneaux aux Morilles in my own kitchen I knew there was nothing I couldn't make if I put my mind to it and had the right ingredients. It helps to have a friend who had the ear of so many chefs. But most chefs are generous and if you are interested in their food they will pull up a chair and talk to you all night long. It's lonely working in a restaurant kitchen so if you have a favorite chef let them know how much you like their food. I'll bet they come out of the kitchen to meet you.

PIGEONNEAUX AUX MORILLES

Squab Breasts with Morel Sauce

Adrienne first made Pigeonneaux aux Morilles in 1967. Over the years she played with the balance of the sauce until it was absolute perfection. The name does not begin to explain how utterly sublime and delicious this dish is. You will literally lick your plate!

Buy the squabs whole and either remove the breasts yourself or have the butcher do it. Reserve the remainder of the bird, discarding the skin, to make the stock. Adrienne often made the morels, stock, and sauce well in advance in order to let the flavors develop. Steamed potatoes work beautifully to absorb the sauce without being assertive. If you own a *pomme vapeur*, it makes the best steamed potatoes, if not, use a regular steamer.

Serves 4

Prep/cook time: morels 1½ hours; sauce 1 hour; squab 20 minutes

Morilles

32 ounces (4 cups) beef broth (not homemade stock, use store-bought broth)

1 bouquet garni*

3 to 4 ounces dried morel mushrooms

1 tablespoon unsalted butter

1 to 2 cups heavy cream

In a saucepan, combine the beef broth and bouquet garni; bring to a boil. Add the dried morels, cover, and remove from the heat. Steep for 1 hour. Strain through cheesecloth, reserving the liquid. Rinse the morels well under tap water to make sure no grit or sand remains. Set aside the liquid.

Over medium heat, melt the butter in a saucepan and add the morels. Swirl until they are coated with the butter, then sauté gently for 2 to 3 minutes. Add enough cream to almost cover. Bring to a boil, lower the heat, and simmer gently, stirring occasionally, until most of the cream is absorbed and what remains is thickened, about 45 minutes. While the morels are simmering, start the sauce.

Sauce

1/3 cup vermouth

2 tablespoons Glace de Viande (page 25)

Scant 2 cups heavy cream

1 tablespoon plus 1 to 2 teaspoons Beurre Manié (page 35)

6 tablespoons Madeira or calvados

1 cup morilles liquid

1 cup Squab or Chicken Stock (page 23)

Salt and freshly ground black pepper

1 tablespoon Caneton en Papillotte sauce (page 107), optional

In a saucepan over medium-high heat, reduce the vermouth and glace de viande by half. Add one-third cup of cream and reduce again by half. Add 1 tablespoon beurre manié and cook for 15 minutes. Set the vermouth reduction aside.

In a saucepan, heat the Madeira over high heat until almost simmering. Flame the Madeira by igniting the alcohol in the steam coming off the Madeira with a match or gas lighter. Allow all the alcohol to burn off, swirling the pan while it does so. The flames will subside when all the alcohol has burned off. Removing the alcohol tempers the taste of the Madeira so that it does not overwhelm the sauce. Add ½ cup of the morel soaking liquid, the squab stock, and 1½ cups cream. Simmer until reduced by one-third. Taste and add salt and pepper, ½ cup of the morel liquid, and 1 teaspoon beurre manié. Simmer gently until reduced again by one-third. If using, add the Caneton en Papillotte

continued

sauce and simmer 5 minutes. If you are not using the Caneton en Papillotte sauce you may need to add another teaspoon beurre manié to thicken the sauce.

Add the morels and their cream and simmer gently for 5 minutes. Taste and correct for seasoning. You should have a strong morel taste, but now with the subtle nuance of the squab stock. Now add just half of the vermouth reduction. Simmer gently. Taste. The vermouth reduction is slightly sweet so you must determine for yourself if you should add more. You can add by tablespoons until the taste is right for you. I usually use just a bit more than half of the reduction at this point, and then add a bit more after adding the livers below. There is no way to be exact because it all depends on the strength of the mushrooms, the squab stock, and the livers. At this point, the morels and sauce can be cooled and refrigerated for up to a week. Bring to room temperature before reheating.

Potatoes and Squab

12 fingerling potatoes of similar size

1 tablespoon sunflower oil

2 tablespoons unsalted butter

Boneless breasts from 4 squabs and their livers (or use chicken livers), at room temperature

¼ cup plus 2 tablespoons Madeira or calvados

Peel the potatoes and cut into uniform chunks. In a *pomme vapeur* or steamer, cook until they just about fall apart, 20 to 25 minutes, depending on their size. Keep warm.

Heat the sunflower oil and butter in a sauté pan over medium-high heat. Add the squab breasts, sauté for 4 to 5 minutes. Turn them for an additional 3 to 4 minutes; they should still be rare in the center but not raw. Be careful not to overcook the breast meat, it goes from red to gray in a matter of minutes and they will continue cooking while they rest. Remove to a warm plate.

In the same pan, sauté the livers until just gray on the outside and reddish inside, about 5 minutes. Remove the livers and deglaze the pan with a scant ¼ cup Madeira, scraping up any crusty bits from the pan. Add back the livers and mash them into the liquid. Add the livers to the morel sauce in thirds, tasting after every addition. If the sauce becomes too strong, add the remaining vermouth reduction by tablespoons.

Over medium heat, add the squab and remaining 2 tablespoons Madeira to the pan. Ignite the Madeira and swirl the contents until the flames subside. Remove the breasts to a warm platter and add the liquid to the sauce. Taste the sauce and correct seasoning, you may need a drop of white wine vinegar or Champagne vinegar to brighten it. Place two squab breasts on each plate along with the potatoes. Dress the squab with the sauce and morels. Crush the potatoes with the back of a spoon into the sauce.

See page 146

MICHEL GUÉRARD
Les Prés d'Eugénie by way of Le Pot-au-Feu

In 1971 Andre Surmain, co-owner of Lutèce in New York City, came back from Paris raving about a tiny little two-star restaurant in an industrial suburb of Paris. M. Surmain made a reservation for Adrienne and her husband and off they went on a food odyssey which resulted in a lifelong friendship with Michel Guérard, and his wife Christine.

The restaurant was called Le Pot-au-Feu, which translates as "pot on the fire," and references a quintessential French dish, popular with rich and poor, in the country and city, that is the essence of French home cooking. True to the tradition of the dish for which it was named, you entered the restaurant through the back door past the coat rack and the postage stamp-sized kitchen. The tables were so close together that in order to sit down or get up the entire row in which your table was located needed to move. On that first visit, they found themselves in good company when they sat down next to Julia Child and her husband.

Thanks to Adrienne's obsessive note-taking we know that Michel discussed the menu with them and chose the desserts. He trained as a pastry chef and won the prestigious Meilleur Ouvrier de France for Pastry in 1958. See her notes about the meal on the next page.

Le Pot-au-Feu was forced to close in 1972 because a new road was cutting straight through the restaurant. But Adrienne followed Michel when he resurfaced in 1974 at the spa at Eugénie-les-Bain. Over the course of more than 40 years, and hundreds of meals, a friendship took hold that bridged the divide between chef and patron.

DINNER MAY 1971
Le Pot-au-Feu

Foie Gras de Maison excellent, delicate and delicious no gelee. (16)

Saumon frais aux ciboulettes *thin escalope of salmon sautéed, served in a lovely light sauce with chopped chives.* (16)

Merlan Braise après F. Point *carrots, onions and lots of mushrooms all sort of covering the whole, boned whiting; sauce was faintly sweet and exquisite – delicate, tres raffine.* (19)

Aileron de Volaille aux concombres *Just incredible! Succulent bits of chicken done en casserole with little wedges of cucumber (+ other vegetables) in a light sauce – just delectable.* (19)

Charolaise a la moele Fleurie *excellent straight-forward Charolaise, bordelaise sauce.* (16)

Pommes Anna *very thinly sliced potato, crusty and brown on top - delicious.* (16)

Wine: *Sancerre 18 Fr and Brouilly (served in a cold pewter tankard/carafe) 15 Fr*

Feuillete aux poires caramelise *a wonderful light square of feuillete filled with cr. Chantilly, on top a whole pear sliced in very thin slices and caramelized – just divine... soft and creamy, crisp and crunchy all at the same time.* (18)

La Dijionaise cassis sorbet, *small pieces of pear & poire eau de vie – a lovely combination.* (17)

Adrienne and Michel Guerard at Mondavi Kitchen, Napa Valley, CA

VOLAILLE AU MEURSAULT ET AUX CONCOMBRES

Chicken and Cucumbers in White Wine Sauce

The combination of chicken and cucumbers was something Adrienne had never encountered before she tasted this dish at Michel Guérard's first restaurant, Le Pot-au-Feu outside of Paris. Indeed, it was classic Guérard to elegantly marry two unlikely flavors and textures, creating something sublime yet not overwrought. I love that the sauce is very much like the Jus Lié, page 36! The original recipe calls for chicken wings, blanched and deboned. I think thighs have more flavor and are less work. It is important to note that the butter must be foaming before adding the cucumbers, otherwise they will take too long to brown and taste sour. The Pommes Anna (page 62) is a perfect side dish.

Serves 4

Prep/cook time: 1 hour

3 tablespoons unsalted butter

4 skinless boneless chicken thighs (salted 1 hour or up to 24 hours in advance; see page 141)

Salt and freshly ground black pepper

1 tablespoon finely chopped shallot

3 ounces fresh mushrooms, finely chopped

3 tablespoons dry vermouth

½ cup dry white wine

¾ cup heavy cream

2 tablespoons peeled, seeded and chopped tomatoes, fresh or canned

¼ teaspoon chopped fresh tarragon

1½ teaspoons chopped fresh Italian flat-leaf parsley

2 cucumbers (about 10 ounces total)

½ teaspoon sugar

Heat 2 tablespoons of butter in a sauté pan over medium-high heat. Add the chicken and season with pepper. Cook for about 10 minutes on each side, until lightly browned. Remove the chicken to a plate and add the shallot and mushrooms to the pan. Sauté about 3 minutes, until softened. Pour off any excess fat. Add the vermouth and white wine and reduce until almost all the liquid has evaporated. Add cream, tomatoes, tarragon, and half the parsley. Simmer until reduced by half. Return the chicken to the sauce, lower the heat, and simmer until cooked through, about 10 minutes.

Meanwhile, in a saucepan, bring 4 cups water to boil with 1 tablespoon salt. Peel the cucumbers, quarter lengthwise, and deseed. Cut each quarter into four pieces of uniform length. Drop them in the boiling water and blanch for 3 minutes. Drain on paper towels.

In a sauté pan, heat the remaining 1 tablespoon butter over high heat until foaming and golden brown. Add the cucumbers and brown lightly on both sides, about 2 minutes. Sprinkle with the sugar and sauté for 2 minutes longer, until golden brown. Drain on paper towels. Place the chicken and sauce on the serving plates, top with the cucumbers, and sprinkle with the remaining parsley.

POULET SAUCE AGRO DOLCE

Sweet and Sour Chicken Fricassee

This unusual but easy dish will wake up your taste buds with a mix of *agro dolce* (tart and sweet), a signature of Troisgros cooking. The recipe comes from a cooking course Jean Troisgros taught at the Mondavi Vineyards in the Napa Valley in 1976. Adrienne was instrumental in Jean agreeing to do the cooking course, and she assisted Jean in the kitchen on that and many subsequent trips he made to the U.S. before his untimely death in 1983.

You may be surprised at the amount of vinegar in this recipe. It is a hallmark of the cuisine of the Troisgros brothers, two of the founders of nouvelle cuisine. The tomatoes add a nice counterbalance of sweetness so don't be afraid of trying the recipe, you will be pleasantly surprised.

The first time I made this, I used elephant garlic but the cloves were enormous and they did not cook thoroughly in the amount of time allowed. I recommend that you use medium-sized cloves so they cook through, then you can easily purée them when pushing them through the sieve into the sauce.

Sweet vegetables like roasted carrots and parsnips or potatoes are a perfect foil to the *agro dolce* sauce. Alternatively, you can make it a bit more Middle Eastern and serve the chicken and its sauce over couscous with a bit of chopped fresh cilantro instead of chervil, and roasted eggplant with a bit of yogurt on the side.

Serves 4

Prep time: 1¼ hours

8 (3-ounce) bone-in chicken thighs, or 2 (6-ounce) bone-in breasts and 4 thighs (salted 1 hour or up to 24 hours in advance; see page 142)

4 tablespoons unsalted butter

1 tablespoon sunflower oil

10 medium cloves garlic, unpeeled

1 cup white wine vinegar

2 fresh tomatoes or 2 canned Italian Plum tomatoes, roughly chopped

1 tablespoon tomato passata, or
    the sauce from the canned
    tomatoes, or plain tomato
    sauce

Bouquet garni*

2 cups Chicken Stock (page 23)

Freshly ground black pepper

Handful fresh chervil or Italian
    flat-leaf parsley, chopped

In a large pan that will hold all the chicken pieces, heat 1 tablespoon of the butter and the oil. Add the chicken pieces and cook, turning, until browned on both sides, 10 to 15 minutes. Add the unpeeled garlic. Place a lid over the pan and continue cooking the thighs for about 20 minutes (just 10 minutes for breasts), until the chicken is cooked through. Cooking the chicken under a domed lid creates an oven-like environment, which cooks the chicken with the moistness of the oil.

Remove the chicken pieces and pour off the excess fat from the pan. Return the pan to the heat and deglaze with the vinegar. Add half of the chopped tomatoes, the passata, and the bouquet garni. Allow the liquid to reduce, uncovered, over gentle heat for 5 to 10 minutes.

Add the chicken stock and reduce by half over medium-high heat, about 20 minutes.

Remove the garlic cloves from their paper and return them to the sauce. Strain the sauce through a sieve into a pan that will be able to accommodate the chicken, forcing the cloves of garlic through the strainer. Barely simmering the sauce over medium heat, beat in the remaining 3 tablespoons butter and the remaining chopped tomato. Taste and season with salt and pepper

Return the chicken to the sauce to warm briefly and sprinkle with the chervil or parsley just before serving.

---

* See page 146

POLLO AL LIMONE CON ROSMARINO E PATATE

Lemon-Rosemary Chicken and Potatoes

When this recipe from Ed Giobbi, author of *Italian Family Cooking*, appeared in *House & Garden* magazine in the early seventies, Adrienne quickly made it her own. It became a mainstay in her repertoire, especially when she had to cook for a crowd, as she often did on weekends at her husband's family home on Long Island.

The original recipe called for using whole rosemary branches, but during the braise the needles disperse into the sauce and are tough and unappealing in the finished dish. I struggled with how to get around this and still keep it a fairly easy dish. In the end I got my resident chopper – my husband – to mince the rosemary. It works perfectly. You might want to mince more than is required for the recipe and freeze it; you don't have to thaw it before using.

I also added leeks and a lemon rind, which work with the chicken and rosemary flavors. Don't use a lemon with the juice in it because the juice will inhibit the cooking of the potatoes. The rind adds a surprising bite to the dish. To make it a complete one-dish meal, I toss in Chantenay baby carrots. They keep the dish easy because they are already the perfect size and don't need peeling or chopping. If you can't find Chantenay carrots, use whole carrots but you may need to cut out the tough woody center.

Serves 6 to 8

Prep/cook time: 1 ½ hours

¼ cup olive oil

3 tablespoons unsalted butter

6 cloves garlic, unpeeled

4 (3-ounce) bone-in chicken thighs and 4 (6-ounce) bone-in breasts (salted 1 hour or up to 24 hours in advance; see page 142)

4 leeks, white and a bit of the green, sliced ¼ inch thick

2 cups white wine

10 sprigs fresh rosemary, leaves picked and finely minced

2 bay leaves

1 juiced lemon rind (seeds removed), cut into eighths

10 medium potatoes, sliced ¼ inch thick (Yukon Gold or similar, peeled or not)

Freshly ground black pepper

12 ounces Chantenay carrots, ends trimmed, optional

1 cup Chicken Stock (page 23), as needed

Preheat the oven to 350°F.

Select a casserole that can later be used in the oven (or sauté everything on the stove in a skillet and then transfer to a foil pan for the oven cooking). In the casserole, heat the olive oil and butter over moderate heat. Add the garlic cloves and just the chicken thighs, skin side down, and cook until lightly browned. Turn the thighs and add the breasts. Cook until all pieces are lightly browned on both sides. Season with pepper.

Add the leeks and cook until lightly colored, about 10 minutes, but don't let them burn. Add the wine, rosemary, bay leaves, and lemon. Cover and simmer for 5 minutes. Uncover, raise the heat, and boil rapidly until the wine has reduced by half. Remove the chicken to a warm platter. Add the potatoes and carrots to the pan and season with salt and pepper. Add enough stock to cover the vegetables. Bring to a simmer on the stove.

Cover and slide into the oven. Bake the vegetables, stirring occasionally, for 30 minutes. Add the thighs and any juice that has exuded from them and bake for 10 minutes. Add the breasts; the potatoes will break up and you should even encourage this when you stir the mixture. Cook for another 10 minutes, until the chicken is cooked through and the sauce has thickened. Add additional stock as needed; the sauce should not be soupy but the dish should be moist. Remove and discard the bay leaves. Take out the garlic, remove the skins, then crush the cooked garlic back into the sauce.

If your sauce is too soupy, remove the chicken and boil the liquid furiously on the stove until you get the right texture and taste.

You can make the dish ahead and refrigerate for a week to 10 days. To reheat in the oven: Remove the chicken pieces and add stock to the sauce if necessary – the potatoes will have absorbed quite a bit of the liquid. Warm in a 300°F oven for 15 minutes. Add the chicken pieces and heat for 10 minutes longer.

CANETON EN PAPILLOTTE

Duck Breasts with Provençal Herbs

This earthy, rich, Provençal method for cooking duck comes from André Lalleman, the patron at Auberge de Noves (formerly La Petite Auberge) in Noves near Avignon. Adrienne had this dish on a number of occasions in the restaurant, so when the recipe was published she was delighted. But, as so often happens, the published recipe didn't quite work. When Adrienne cornered M. Lalleman on her next visit he confessed that the published recipe wasn't complete and gave her the missing elements. "Restaurant" recipes are often modified to accommodate the perceived abilities of the home cook, or the availability of ingredients, or to prevent others from replicating signature dishes. But in every case, when Adrienne pointed out the discrepancy between her results at home and the restaurant's, they were first impressed and then eager to clarify the recipe for her.

This sauce is always in my freezer because it works so well with other game birds and poultry. Adrienne always made double the quantity and used it to add a mysterious zing to her sauces. It is not difficult to make, but forcing the herb mixture through the sieve is a bit time consuming. If you are not able to find some of the herbs – in particular chervil and savory can be difficult to locate – increase the quantity of the other herbs proportionally. Cooking the duck skin separately, like pork cracklings, is my own addition because I hate to see it wasted. Serve with steamed potatoes and the Haricots Vert avec Marjolaine et Ciboulettes on page 66 for a truly Provençal meal.

Serves 4

Prep/cook time: sauce 2 hours; duck and cracklings 40 minutes

Sauce

½ cup chopped fresh Italian flat-leaf parsley

3 tablespoons minced fresh rosemary

2½ teaspoons chopped fresh marjoram

3 tablespoons dried thyme

3½ teaspoons dried savory

2 teaspoons dried chervil

2½ teaspoons dried sage

1½ teaspoons dried oregano

½ cup raw duck or chicken livers, roughly chopped

⅔ cup chopped shallots, about 3 small shallots

10 cloves garlic, chopped

2½ cups white wine

2½ tablespoons strong Dijon mustard

¾ cup (1½ sticks) unsalted butter, melted

2 heaping teaspoons Beurre Manié (page 35), plus extra as needed

1 tablespoon cassis, optional

Salt and freshly ground black pepper

Cracklings and Duck

4 boneless duck breasts (salted 1 hour or up to 24 hours in advance; see page 142), skin removed and reserved

Sunflower oil

Sauce

Combine the fresh and dried herbs in a food processor until pulverized. Add the livers, shallots, and garlic. Process until the mixture is liquid. Force the mixture through a fine sieve into a saucepan. You should have about ½ cup of dried herbs that will not pass through; reserve them to use later in the sauce.

Add the white wine, mustard, melted butter, beurre manié, and optional cassis to the pan. Cook over medium heat, stirring occasionally, until the sauce thickens, about 15 to 20 minutes. Correct the seasoning for salt (lots) and pepper, and the texture by adding some reserved herbs and additional beurre manié as needed. You want a somewhat grainy mixture that when cooled becomes a paste (due to the flour in the beurre manié and the cooked liver).

Cracklings

Preheat the oven to 350°F.

At least an hour before cooking the duck, cut the duck skin into strips about 1-inch wide. Coat a ceramic cast-iron baking dish with a light film of oil. Place the skin strips in the pan and roast for 20 minutes, until the skin is crisp and all the fat has rendered. Remove the skin to drain on paper towels. Keep warm. Save the rendered fat for roasting potatoes.

Duck

Lay out four sheets of buttered foil large enough to wrap each duck breast. Place a spoonful of sauce on each piece and place a duck breast on top. Place another spoon of sauce on top of each duck breast. Bring the long edges of the foil to meet and crimp or fold them over tightly just until the fold is close to the top of each breast but not touching. Crimp or fold the short ends.

Place the packets in a single layer in a shallow baking pan and bake for 15 minutes. Carefully open one foil package to check the cooking. The duck is done when the meat at the center of the breast bounces back. Or use a small knife to cut a slit in one breast – it should be red but not raw. They will continue cooking while they rest and the lean meat can go from pink to overcooked in a matter of minutes. If they are raw, return to oven for 3 to 5 minutes. Allow to rest out of the oven in the foil for 5 minutes.

Pour the juices from each foil package into the sauce in the pan. Heat gently. Slice the duck breasts on the diagonal and plate with the sauce, potatoes, and cracklings. Serve additional sauce in a bowl along with the duck. Freeze any unused sauce and strained herb mixture.

La Carte

Champagne - René Lalou 1969

- - - - - - - - - - - - - -

Coquilles à la nage
  Meursault Hospice de Beaune
        1966
  Cuvée Goureau - Drouhin

Entrecôte aux Épinards
  Musigny - Comte de Vogüé
        1959

Salade
Fromage

La Fantasie Davoise

Café

Jeudi 26 Octobre 1978

MORE THAN MEAT

Red meat is not bad for you. Now, blue-green meat, that's bad for you!

— Tom Smothers

Adrienne was quite fond of unusual meat and game or unusual preparations of ordinary meat. But she was also happy with a really good hamburger and a beer. Her husband, however, was diagnosed with high cholesterol very early in his life and the medical advice at the time was to restrict meat. They were willing to follow that advice on most occasions but when they decided to splurge they really went all out.

Foie gras, served hot like calves' liver but worlds away in terms of taste and delicacy, was a favorite dish for special occasions. The steak and baby spinach is a classic Troisgros recipe with lots of vinegar but it couldn't be simpler to make and was often our choice for a quick Friday night meal. Moussaka, well what can I say about fried eggplant, ground beef or lamb, tomato sauce, and cheese except it is a lot of work and it is worth it! Finally, there are the grilled kidneys with a Bordelaise sauce. If you don't like kidneys you won't like this dish but have a go with the Bordelaise sauce, it is quite versatile. If you do like kidneys you will be in heaven!

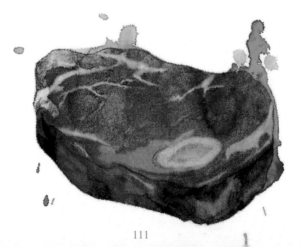

ESCALOPE DE FOIE GRAS À LA VINAIGRETTE

Foie Gras with Vinaigrette

This is a classic nouvelle cuisine dish which Adrienne first tasted at Girardet in 1976 (see page 133). She quickly learned to re-create it at home. It's easy and elegant – the best combination. We often made it for dinner on New Year's Eve as a very special way to begin the year. You can serve it as a starter for four or as a main for two, but make sure whoever you are serving it to is very, very deserving.

Fresh foie gras can be ordered online or purchased in specialty stores. Be sure that you get a fresh uncooked slice, not a pâté or terrine. Like most livers, when you cook the foie gras it will exude a lot of fat, which is why you cook it dry, without the addition of oil, in a nonstick pan.

Serves 2

Prep/cook time: 30 minutes

1 shallot, minced

2½ tablespoons white wine vinegar

Salt and freshly ground black pepper

2½ tablespoons walnut oil

2 slices fresh foie gras, about 5 ounces each and ½ inch thick (see Note)

1 to 2 tablespoons all-purpose flour

3 ounces fresh arugula

2 tablespoons chopped mixed fresh chervil, parsley, and chives

In a small saucepan, cook the shallot, vinegar, salt, and pepper over medium-high heat for 1 to 2 minutes. Whisk in the walnut oil. Remove from the heat but keep warm.

Salt and pepper each slice of foie gras and flour lightly. Heat a nonstick sauté pan over high heat. Add the foie slices to the dry skillet and sear for 30 seconds each side. Drain the foie gras on paper towels, then place on warmed plates.

Scatter arugula around the foie gras. Whisk the chervil, parsley, and chives into the warm vinaigrette, then drizzle over the foie gras and arugula.

Note: You can purchase slices of foie gras or a whole lobe, online from specialty retailers like D'Artagnan. If you are using a whole lobe, you can slice two ½-inch thick slices from it. For a main course, two slices will be perfect for two people. As an appetizer, cut each slice in half again for four people. If you are not using the whole lobe, you can freeze the remainder for up to a month. The foie gras will shrink quite a bit during cooking.

ENTRECÔTE AU VINAIGRE ET EPINARD

Steak with Spinach and Vinegar Dressing

This Jean Troisgros recipe pays tribute to the ingredients, so find the best quality steak and baby spinach you can afford. It is another example of his signature use of vinegar for a bright contrasting taste.

Serves 2

Prep/cook time: 45 minutes

5 shallots

¼ cup sherry vinegar

¾ cup red wine vinegar

3 cups red wine

1 cup tomato sauce or passata (uncooked tomato puree)

Salt and freshly ground black pepper

1 egg

8 ounces baby spinach, washed and dried

Handful fresh Italian flat-leaf parsley and tarragon, chopped

3 to 4 tablespoons unsalted butter

12 to 14 ounces New York strip steak, bavette (aka flap steak) or skirt steak, cut into ½-inch-thick slices (salted 1 hour or up to 24 hours in advance; see page 142)

Finely chop three shallots. In a saucepan, combine shallots, sherry and red wine vinegars, red wine, tomato sauce and a little salt and pepper. Simmer until reduced by half, about 20 minutes. Taste for seasoning. Strain.

Meanwhile, prick the round end of the egg shell with a pin. Place in a small saucepan and add enough cold water to cover it by about ¼ inch. Bring to a boil, reduce the heat, and simmer for 7 minutes. Immediately drain off the hot water and place the pan under cold running tap water for about 1 minute. Turn off the tap and leave the egg in the cold water until it is cool enough to handle, about 2 minutes. This method prevents the green color and dark rings around the yolk. Peel; put the yolk through a sieve and finely chop the white.

In a saucepan place a tablespoon of vinegar dressing and the spinach. Cover and place over low heat. Spinach is mostly water and will turn to mush if you cook it in water. Once the spinach is wilted and reduced - about 5 minutes – remove to a colander and press hard to force the water out. Place the empty pan on low heat to dry. Add the spinach, tarragon and parsley. Toss to combine and turn off the heat but keep warm.

In a large skillet over high heat, melt 2 tablespoons of butter. When the butter is foaming, add the steak slices and cook for about 2 minutes each side, until just seared on the outside but quite rare on the inside. Cook the steak in batches if necessary. If you crowd the slices into the pan they will steam rather than sear. Do not overcook or the steak will be tough. Remove to a warm plate, where the meat will continue cooking for a bit.

Chop the remaining 2 shallots. Reduce the heat under the pan to medium, add the shallots, and cook just until softened. Add some of the vinegar dressing to deglaze the pan then pour the contents into the vinegar dressing. Put the dressing on medium heat and when warmed whisk in the remaining 1 to 2 tablespoons butter; taste for seasoning, salt, pepper, or even lemon juice. Arrange the spinach on two warm plates, lay the steak strips on top, and ladle a generous amount of the vinegar dressing over them. Sprinkle with the chopped egg yolk and white and sea salt.

MOUSSAKA

At the end of the summer when the eggplants came fast, furious, and enormous, we made moussaka by the trayful. The whole family gathered round to lend a hand in the preparations. But in reality we were all waiting for a taste of that first batch of fried eggplant, hot and melting in the middle – it's the best part of making moussaka. Of course the finished product was devoured as well, but that taste of fried eggplant hot from the skillet is the reason we always begged Adrienne, "Please make moussaka!"

You must salt the eggplant slices in order to draw the water out or they will not fry properly. If you don't, the liquid they exude will make the moussaka soupy and bitter. And it is helpful to have two pans for frying the eggplant and two people manning them. If your kitchen is big enough and you have enough friends/family, a third person can make the meat sauce. When I do it solo, it takes the best part of an afternoon, so to make the time truly worth it, I usually make double the quantity, one for dinner and one for the freezer. I cut the moussaka destined for the freezer into quarters and freeze each section separately. Countless times I have been delighted to find this delicious homemade dish in my freezer when I was too tired to cook.

(Exact amounts are meaningless; more or less of this or that – it doesn't matter. When putting bottom layer of eggplant in pan – overlap to make a solid base – next layer can have spaces in it) MOUSSAKA – *(enough for 8)*

Serves 8

Prep time: 2 hours. Assembly and cook time: 1¼ hours

4 to 6 medium to large eggplants
Salt
½ cup all-purpose flour
Sunflower oil
1 tablespoon olive oil
1 medium onion, finely chopped
2 cloves garlic, chopped
1½ pounds ground beef or lamb
¼ pound ground pork
¼ pound ground veal
2 ripe tomatoes or two canned Italian tomatoes, peeled and chopped

1 (16-ounce) bottle tomato sauce
4 tablespoons fresh oregano
2 tablespoons dried oregano
2 tablespoons fresh or dried thyme
Freshly ground black pepper
12 ounces shredded mild cheeses, perhaps 8 ounces fontina and 4 ounces Cheddar
4 eggs
1½ cups light cream

Eggplant

Slice the eggplant into ½-inch-thick slices. Sprinkle with lots of salt on both sides, lay on paper towels, and let sit for 20 to 30 minutes. Remove to fresh paper towels and press lightly to remove as much water as possible. Place the flour on a plate. Heat ¼ inch sunflower oil in a large skillet over medium-high heat until just smoking. Don't add more than a ¼ inch of oil because the eggplant absorbs a lot of the oil in the pan and it will taste greasy. In batches, dredge the eggplant slices in the flour, shake off excess, and place in the hot oil. Brown on both sides, 8 to 10 minutes, remove to paper towels to drain. Continue until all the eggplant is fried.

Important: The flour that remains in the pan will start to burn after about two batches and will make everything taste bitter. Pour out the oil and wipe the pan with a paper towel – being careful not to burn yourself – and continue with fresh oil. Also, do not dredge the eggplant in the flour until you are ready to put it in the oil. If you do it too far in advance, the eggplant will soak up the flour and not fry properly.

Meat Sauce

Heat the olive oil in a large skillet over medium-high heat. Add the onion and garlic and sauté until softened. Add all the ground meats and cook, stirring and breaking up the meat, until browned and crumbly. Drain off excess fat and water. Return the pan to the heat and add the tomatoes, tomato sauce, fresh oregano, dried oregano, thyme, salt, and pepper. Reduce the heat to medium and simmer for 20 minutes, until cooked through.

Assembly

Preheat the oven to 350°F

Lightly oil a 13 x 9-inch baking pan or 3-quart casserole. Layer the eggplant slices, then the meat sauce, then the cheese in the casserole until all the ingredients have been used, about 3 layers each. End with a layer of cheese. Beat together the eggs and cream until smooth. Pour over the casserole. Bake for 45 minutes, until browned and bubbly. Cool for 10 minutes before serving.

ROGNON DE VEAU GRILLE BORDELAISE

Grilled Veal Kidneys in Bordelaise

This recipe is for those who love veal kidneys as they are front and center. Adrienne first had rognon de veau at Girardet, and after a long discussion with Frédy Girardet, she made it at home for New Year's Eve 1976. We have since made it together and separately and it is always sublime.

Bordelaise sauce is simply made from reduced veal stock and good red wine. It is not complicated or difficult. Adrienne's recipe from 1976 indicated she used a Corton Clos du Roi 1961 – a wine from Burgundy! But we generally use a very good Côtes du Rhône. If you have made the demi-glace on page 25, you can use 2 cups of that instead of making Adrienne's light veal stock below (which eliminates roasting the bones and just simmers on the stove for 6 to 7 hours). Make the stock and sauce a day or a week ahead. It is also important to get the best-quality veal kidneys since they will be the star of the dish. The Pommes Anna on page 62 would be sublime as a side dish.

Serves 2

Prep/cook time: stock 6–7 hours; sauce 45 minutes; kidneys 25 minutes

Veal Stock

2 pounds veal shank bones, cut into 2-inch sections

10 to 12 ounces veal breast

2 whole white onions, peeled and stuck with one whole clove each

1 whole carrot

1 stalk celery, cut in half

Bouquet garni*

8 cups water

1½ tablespoons Glace de Viande (page 25 or use store-bought)

Bordelaise

2 cups very good red Côtes du Rhône

1 teaspoon Beurre Manié (page 35)

1 to 2 tablespoons unsalted butter, cut into pieces

Veal Stock

Combine the veal bones and breast, onion, carrot, celery, bouquet garni, and water in a stockpot and bring to a boil. Reduce the heat and simmer for 6 to 7 hours, adding additional water if necessary. Strain through a sieve. Return to the heat, add the glace de viande, and reduce by half, to about 2 cups.

Bordelaise Sauce

Combine the veal stock and red wine in a saucepan. Bring to a simmer and reduce by half. Off heat, whisk in the beurre manié, then simmer for 10 to 15 minutes, until the paste has been incorporated. Correct for seasoning. Beat in 1 to 2 tablespoons butter just before serving.

continued

Kidney

12 ounces veal kidney

2 tablespoons unsalted butter, melted

1 tablespoon unsalted butter

1 shallot, minced

1 clove garlic, minced

1 cup fresh breadcrumbs

1 teaspoon mustard

Preheat the oven to 500°F.

Cut the kidney into thirds without cutting through any of the lobes. If you examine the kidney you will see a logical way to cut around the lobes. Remove as much as possible of the white membrane on the underside of the kidney. You will not be able to remove it all because it holds the kidney together.

Place the sectioned kidney on a rack in a roasting pan. Brush with the melted butter. Place in the upper third of the oven and roast for 3 minutes. Turn the pieces and roast another 3 minutes, until lightly browned. Remove and drain on paper towels. Reduce the oven temperature to 400°F.

Heat the 1 tablespoon butter in a sauté pan over medium heat. When it is foaming, add the shallot and garlic and cook until softened. Remove from the heat and add the breadcrumbs, mustard, and a teaspoon of the bordelaise sauce. Stir to combine.

Remove the rack from the roasting pan and line the pan with aluminum foil. Pat half of the breadcrumb mixture on the underside of the kidneys. Place the kidneys on the roasting pan and pat remaining breadcrumb mixture on top. Place the roasting pan on the center rack of the oven and roast for 5 minutes, or until breadcrumbs are browned. Remove and wrap the foil loosely around the kidneys and let them to rest for 3 minutes while finishing the sauce.

Finish the sauce by whisking in the 1 to 2 tablespoons butter. If there are drippings from the kidneys, add them to the sauce. Place the kidneys on warmed plates, making sure all the breadcrumbs from underneath go with them, and dress with the bordelaise sauce.

---

* See page 146

La Carte

Mousseline de Saumon
Beurre Blanc

Le Caneton en Papillote
mode de La Petite Auberge

Pommes Vapeur

Salade
La Fantasie Danoise

Chevalier Montrachet — Chambolle Musigny
1961   1929

4/7/6

DESSERT LESS SWEET

All I really need is love, but a little chocolate now and then doesn't hurt.

— Charles Schulz (as Lucy Van Pelt)

When I first started cooking with Adrienne, she made the first course, the main course, and the sauce. I made the dessert, usually something involving pastry. Even though I was the acknowledged Pastry Queen, Adrienne was teaching me to taste carefully and respect the essence of the ingredients. I had had a heavy hand with sugar in the beginning, but as I started to pull back on it, the natural sweetness and flavor of the ingredients were allowed to shine. It is almost impossible to taste as you go with dessert, but the more I baked for Adrienne, the less I depended on added sugar.

Long before I came on the scene though, Adrienne had her own repertoire of desserts. Most of them were directly or indirectly inspired by the chefs and "new" cuisine that was informing all of her other cooking. These dessert recipes all share certain critical elements: Most can be made in advance, are light in taste, and have the right balance of sweetness. The last thing you taste in a meal shouldn't dull your taste buds; it should continue to tantalize them.

I was fascinated by the refreshing bite of Candied Grapefruit and the balance of the sweet pastry and tart plums in the Heavenly Plum Clafoutis. The lightness, yet intensely chocolate taste of the Mocha (Marriage) Mousse had me at first bite. But I think the biggest surprise was the Danish Fantasy – a combination of tart/sweet pineapple and bittersweet chocolate enveloped in a cloud of whipped cream and served in a caramelized tuile cup. I still love an apple pie straight from the oven but these desserts have earned their place in my repertoire.

MOCHA (MARRIAGE) MOUSSE

Adrienne's husband told me that he loved her mocha mousse so much that it tipped the balance in favor of asking Adrienne to marry him. This was not a guy who took marriage, or chocolate, lightly! But after they were married in Paris, he said that Adrienne never made the dessert again!

In her defense, Adrienne had embarked on cooking lessons with Simca Beck just after she married and began making much more elaborate meals, which meant less time to make dessert. She says she'd had no idea how critical the recipe had been to the marriage proposal. When we resurrected it we re-named it Mocha Marriage Mousse. It originally came from *The Around the World Cookbook*, which I cannot find online nor can I locate in Adrienne's library. If anyone has a copy I would love to see the original recipe.

Serves 6

Prep/cook time: 1¼ hours plus 4 hours to chill

3 ounces semisweet or bittersweet chocolate, coarsely chopped

4 egg yolks

¾ cup sugar

3 tablespoons brewed espresso coffee, cooled

1½ teaspoons (⅔ envelope) unflavored gelatin

2 cups heavy cream

3 egg whites

1 ounce shaved or grated semisweet or bittersweet chocolate

Place the chopped chocolate in the top of a double boiler set over simmering water. Stir occasionally until the chocolate is completely melted. Remove the top of the double boiler and set aside to cool while you prepare the rest of the ingredients.

In a standing mixer with the whisk attachment or with an electric beater, beat the egg yolks until light in color. Add the sugar and continue beating until light and fluffy. Add 2 tablespoons of the espresso and the cooled melted chocolate and mix well.

Place the remaining 1 tablespoon espresso in a small cup. Sprinkle the gelatin over and let sit for a minute, until softened. If needed, add 1 teaspoon cream to dissolve the gelatin completely. Stir the gelatin mixture into the chocolate mixture and set aside. The addition of the gelatin helps the mousse hold its light airy texture.

With an electric mixer, whip the cream to soft peaks, then gently fold into chocolate mixture.

In a clean dry bowl, beat the whites until stiff but not dry. Fold one-third slowly and carefully into the chocolate mixture. When it has been incorporated, fold in half the remaining whites. When that has been incorporated, fold in the final portion of whites. The gradual incorporation of the whites helps to preserve the structure of the mousse.

Scrape the mousse into individual glasses or a 2-quart mold. Chill at least 4 hours. Garnish with shaved chocolate.

CLAFOUTIS PRUNEAUX

Adrienne's Heavenly Plum Clafoutis

There are many recipes for clafoutis that are made with whatever fruit is in season. But this one is particularly suited to sour Italian plums because they contrast so perfectly with the pastry, which is quite sweet. Adrienne was not fond of overly sweet desserts; she was always looking for that sweet/sour balance and in this recipe she found it.

Serves 8

Prep/cook time: 1¾ hours

¾ cup (1½ sticks) unsalted butter, at room temperature

1 cup plus 2 tablespoons sugar

1½ cups all-purpose flour

½ teaspoon baking powder

¾ teaspoon ground cinnamon

¾ teaspoon salt

About 1 pound Italian plums, washed, quartered, and pitted

2 eggs

¾ cup heavy cream

In a standing mixer with a paddle attachment, cream the butter until it is white and light. Add the sugar and continue to beat until it is thoroughly incorporated and the mixture is light.

Measure the flour, baking powder, cinnamon, and salt into a bowl and stir to combine. Beating the creamed butter mixture on medium speed, add the flour mixture, 2 tablespoons at a time, fully incorporating the flour between additions. After all the flour is combined, the mixture should just hold together, as a short pastry might feel. Measure out ⅓ cup and set aside.

Transfer the remaining pastry mixture to an ungreased 8-inch spring form pan. Using your fingertips, evenly pat the pastry on the bottom and halfway up the sides of the pan in a very rustic crust. Do not overwork the pastry. Refrigerate for 15 minutes.

Preheat the oven to 375°F.

Arrange the plums in the pastry shell in a single layer in concentric circles, beginning around the outer edge and ending in the center. Do not overlap. Sprinkle the remaining pastry mixture over the plums. Bake for 15 minutes.

Meanwhile, beat the eggs lightly and stir in the cream. Mix well.

Pour the egg/cream mixture over the plums. Return to the oven and bake for 45 to 50 minutes longer, until the top is browned. Test with a knife or toothpick – if it comes out clean it is done. Allow to cool completely. It can sit for 4 to 5 hours. Do not refrigerate immediately.

ROULADE LÉONTINE

Rolled Chocolate Cake

In 1942, an Englishwoman, Dione Lucas, arrived in New York to teach French cooking to an increasingly receptive American audience. In the decades that followed her arrival she founded and ran New York's famous Cordon Bleu restaurant, wrote several successful cookbooks, conducted cooking classes, and became one of the first to teach cooking on a TV series – even before Julia Child!

The dish she was best known for was her chocolate roll Léontine. She first tasted the dessert at a friend's home in upstate New York. It had been made by their French cook, Léontine. Lucas asked for the recipe and published it in *The Gourmet Cooking School Cookbook* in 1964. It became a minor classic and a regular feature on Adrienne's dinner party menus throughout the sixties and seventies. It is a brilliant make-ahead dessert and a real crowd pleaser.

We add cherries or raspberries as a garnish; otherwise the recipe is unchanged. The whole thing can be made hours or a day in advance and kept in the fridge.

Serves 10

Prep/cook/assemble time: 1½ hours

6 eggs, separated

¾ cup sugar

3 tablespoons extra-strong coffee or espresso

6 ounces bittersweet or semisweet chocolate, coarsely chopped

2 teaspoons vanilla extract

Salt

1½ cups heavy cream

Confectioners' sugar for dusting

Cocoa powder for dusting

2 ounces bittersweet chocolate, shaved or roughly chopped

Cherries or raspberries for garnish

Preheat the oven to 350°F.

Butter a 12 x 17½-inch jelly-roll pan or a 1-inch-deep baking sheet, then line with buttered aluminum foil or parchment. The butter on the pan keeps the foil from slipping, the butter on the foil keeps the cake from sticking.

Beat the egg yolks with ½ cup of the sugar until light canary yellow. Remove to a large bowl that will ultimately hold the egg yolks, whites, and chocolate mixture.

Place the coffee in the top of a double boiler over hot but not boiling water. Add the 6 ounces chopped chocolate and stir occasionally until it melts. Remove from the heat. Add the melted chocolate to the egg yolks mixture and stir to incorporate. Stir in 1 teaspoon of the vanilla.

Beat the egg whites with a pinch of salt until just foamy. Still beating, add the remaining ¼ cup sugar, a tablespoon at a time, to form stiff, glossy peaks. Fold one-third of the egg whites into the chocolate/egg yolk mixture. When incorporated, fold in half the remaining egg whites and then the final addition. Do not overwork, but make sure that there are no white blobs remaining.

Pour the batter into the prepared pan and smooth out. Bake for 15 minutes or until a sharp knife inserted comes out clean. Remove from the oven and cover with a clean dish towel that has been dampened with water and thoroughly squeezed out. Allow to sit for 20 minutes, until cool.

Meanwhile, whip the cream in a clean cold bowl to soft peaks. Add the remaining 1 teaspoon vanilla and continue whipping to stiff peaks, but don't let it turn to butter.

Overlap two 12 x 17-inch lengths of aluminum foil to create a rectangle that is a few inches wider than the cake is long (about 20 inches wide). Dust with confectioners' sugar and cocoa in equal parts. Remove the dish towel from the roulade and run a knife along the edges to release it from the foil. Invert it onto the foil with the sugar and cocoa and carefully remove the foil in which it was baked.

Spread the cake with the whipped cream, reserve some for decorating if desired, then top with the 2 ounces shaved/chunked chocolate. Using the foil, roll up the cake from a long side like a jelly roll, and place on a large platter seam side down. Spread a line of whipped cream down the center of the roll and dot with cherries or raspberries if desired. Refrigerate until ready to serve.

FRÉDY GIRARDET

In 1976 rumors were circulating about a new chef who was putting Switzerland on the gastronomic map. Lalou Bize Leroy, owner of Domaine Leroy and shareholder in Romanee-Conti, told Adrienne about an amazing dinner she had in Crissier, Switzerland. Shortly afterwards, Jean Troisgros said "you must go to Girardet in Switzerland I will make the reservation." So they drove 3½ hours from Roanne to Crissier for lunch. When they finished their meal they said "We have to come back!" They made a reservation for dinner in a month's time, because they were renting a house in Mougin, France in the interim.

Frédy Girardet opened his restaurant in 1971 on the ground floor of the city hall building where his father had run a bistro for the locals. He had not planned to follow his father into the restaurant business. In fact, he was hoping to become a professional soccer player but after one meal at Les Frères Troisgros he changed career paths.

Meanwhile, Adrienne and her husband set off from the South of France for their second meal at Girardet in a rental car. Upon arrival at the Swiss border they were turned back by the police because a freak avalanche had closed the road to Genève. What to do? They had a reservation for what they expected to be the meal of a lifetime and the road was closed. Adrienne's husband turned the car around and drove like the wind to the Nice airport. They repacked everything from the car into suitcases, including assorted dried mushrooms, olive oil, and foie gras, and boarded a plane to Geneva. When they landed, they rented a car at the Geneva airport and drove to Crissier, about 30 minutes away. Just remember this was 1976, no cellular phones and no internet with which to make plane and car rental reservations. On the plus side, lots of baggage allowance and no restriction of liquids on airplanes! They arrived at Girardet in time for an aperitif! Dinner was just as amazing as lunch!

LUNCH MAY 1976
Restaurant Girardet

We were seated and given menus then M. Girardet came out of the kitchen followed by a waiter with champagne in a bucket. He sat and had a glass with us – it was Jean's [Troisgros] champagne. He's very warm and charming and at the same time very sure of himself – no modesty visible but also a kind of sweet self-assurance. The result of working a long time and feeling competent, no arrogance at all.

We suggested he decide the menu giving us as many tastes as possible. The first thing was a slice of tarte à l'oignon which we saw some other tables also got but not all. It was a pleasant 1*. But from then on everything was 3***. We were totally knocked out by the delicacy, the nuance, the inventiveness of the guy. He came out after each course to see what we thought!

Foie de Canard au Vinaigre *– Each of us got a medium thick slice of foie seared – really seared and crusted on each side and meltingly tender and pink inside – in a sauce that was a kind of vinaigrette with lots of chopped fines herbs and a haunting nutty flavor that drives me crazy until I figured it out: Huile de Noix. When I asked M. Girardet he said "Bravo!" And that really established our credentials. Jean Troisgros later said it was Huile de Noisette 'plus fin' que Noix and seemed to think the difference was important. The acidity of the vinegar and the nuttiness of the noix combined with the silkiness of the foie was exquisite.* (18)

Brochette de Sole et Saumon à la Menthe *– I don't think we've ever had cooked fish so raw – it was exquisite. Done on a skewer, the taste of each fish was so clean, so fresh and the lightly minted butter sauce a great counterpoint.* (18)

Fricassée de Homard au Truffe *– A classic nouvelle cuisine dish delicately done. Lobster and vegetables in a light buttery sauce with lots of truffles. Excellent delicate taste! All of Girardet's sauces are very "leger"– obviously thickened by a reduction of cream – no flour. The dish was 17 but the lobster claws were 18.* (17)

We drank champagne, then had a ½ bottle Chenin de ? [can't read it] a local wine chosen by Girardet and with the next course a Chateau Leoville Barton.

Pigeon Braise au Chou Vert *– Exquisite – rare, rare, juicy pigeon and the chou was a delicate acid young green chinese cabbage. What a great combination! There was a crispness to the chou which offset the soft rich density of the pigeon. It was glorious.* (18)

Soufflé de Fruit de Passion *- This was the greatest soufflé I've ever had – the silkiest – not creamy – soufflé with a slight tang to it, served with a syrupy acid sauce of the passion fruit that was an exquisite counter point. M.Girardet proudly told us there was no flour in it just eggs, sugar and juice! It had the feeling of a fabulous sabayon and it had risen beautifully above its bowl. I've got to try making it!* (20)

SOUFFLÉ DE PASSION

Passion Fruit Soufflé

Adrienne raved to me about this soufflé long before I had the chance to taste it for myself at Girardet. Even with all that lead up I was still bowled over. It was the first soufflé I learned to make and I have never made any other kind. A soufflé by definition is supposed to be light but this one is ethereal because there is no flour to disguise the sweet/sour taste of the passion fruit which is suspended in a cloud of eggs and sugar.

When you cut open a fresh passion fruit the smell assaults you. It is almost as if you are absorbing the aroma through your taste buds even before the juice hits your mouth. The fruit itself looks a bit like a plum that is very hard and wrinkly on the outside. Inside you find a fibrous web holding the orangey-red seeds which you must strain through a sieve to get the juice. All the while your mouth is puckering.

This is the one dessert that cannot be made in advance. But if you have the oven pre-heated, ramekins chilled, eggs separated, and passion fruit juice and sugar measured, you can make four soufflés in 30 minutes. Do it once and you will be dazzled by the taste and texture.

Serves 4

Prep/cook time: 50 minutes

1 tablespoon butter	½ cup passion fruit juice plus 3 tablespoons
5 eggs, separated	Pinch of salt
⅓ cup plus 3 tablespoons sugar	1 teaspoon honey

Preheat the oven to 450 degrees. Rub the bottom and sides of four individual (1 ¼ cup) soufflé dishes with the butter and refrigerate.

Put the egg yolks in a bowl and add one-third cup of sugar. Beat briskly and well with a wire whisk until pale yellow - 8 to 10 minutes. Add ¼ cup of the passion fruit juice by tablespoons and continue whisking until incorporated.

Beat the egg whites until just barely stiff peaks. Toward the end beat in the remaining three tablespoons of sugar and a pinch of salt.

Fold one third of the whites into the egg yolk mixture. Fold in half the remaining whites and then the final amount. Spoon into the chilled soufflé dishes up to the rim. Using a butter knife sweep across the top to smooth and level the mixture. Place the dishes on a baking sheet on center rack in the oven. Bake 12 minutes until the soufflés have risen halfway above the rim of the dishes.

While the soufflés are cooking, mix the remaining passion fruit juice and honey. Heat for 30 seconds in microwave. Spoon a teaspoon of sauce into the center of each soufflé just before serving.

The only thing that will make a soufflé fall is if it knows you're afraid of it.

— James Beard

FANTAISIE DANOISE

Danish Fantasy

A Danish friend of Adrienne's husband gave her this recipe. It became her go-to dessert for dinner parties beginning in the late sixties right up until I started cooking with her in the nineties. I found it on half a dozen of her handwritten menus, like the one at the beginning of the chapter. Once I tasted the contrast of tart and sweet flavors, I knew why!

The original recipe called for serving it atop almond brittle, but Adrienne felt that was a bit heavy, so we started experimenting with alternatives. We tasted a pastry called *froisses*, which means "crumpled" or "wrinkled," at La Maison Troisgros and thought it might be the solution...but it was too delicate. Finally, we hit on the answer, lace cookies, or *tuiles*. Easy to make, they can be shaped into a bowl or cone to hold the whipped cream, chocolate, and pineapple filling. Don't make them on a rainy or humid day though, or they will be chewy instead of crunchy.

Serves 6

Prep/cook time: 1¾ hours

Tuiles

½ cup (1 stick) unsalted butter

¾ cup packed dark brown sugar

½ cup light corn syrup

1 cup pecans or almonds, finely chopped

6 tablespoons all-purpose flour

¼ teaspoon salt

1 tablespoon heavy cream

1 teaspoon vanilla extract

Filling

2 cups heavy cream

¼ teaspoon vanilla extract

1 envelope (¼ ounce) unflavored gelatin

Half a fresh pineapple, chopped into small chunks

3½ ounces semisweet or bittersweet chocolate, chopped into small pieces

Tuiles

Preheat the oven to 350°F. Line a nonstick baking sheet with a silicone mat or parchment.

In a saucepan over medium heat, combine butter, brown sugar, and corn syrup. Bring to a boil, cook for 5 minutes, stirring frequently. Remove from heat, add nuts, flour, salt, cream, and vanilla. Whisk until smooth.

Drop batter by two rounded tablespoons onto the baking sheet (just two per sheet because the batter will spread quite a bit while baking). Bake for 8 to 10 minutes, until the batter has spread thin and the bubbling has mostly subsided. The tuiles should be dark brown almost caramelized.

Remove from oven and slide the silicone or parchment to a flat surface. Cool for 1 to 2 minutes.

Moving them off the sheet and draping them over the bottom of a small bowl is a bit tricky. Allow yourself a few test tuiles to get the hang of it. They are quite liquid when they come out of the oven but they begin firming up from the outside to the center. Slip a butter knife under a tuile – it's ready when you can slip the knife all the way without tearing the structure. If you wait too long it will be brittle and not malleable. Then, with a spatula, carefully slip it over an upside-down 3-inch bowl or ramekin and mold it to the bowl with your hands.

Repeat with remaining batter to make 6 to 8 tuiles. You'll have enough batter to make about three dozen large tuiles. Store unused batter in an airtight container in the fridge for a few weeks. Store the tuiles, layered between parchment, in an airtight container in a cool, dry place.

Filling

In the bowl of a standing mixer, whip the cream and vanilla until soft peaks form. Mix the gelatin with about a teaspoon warm water until softened. Add to the whipped cream and whip just until combined. Remove the bowl from the mixer and stir in the pineapple and chocolate, reserving six chunks of each for decoration. Refrigerate until ready to assemble. Just before serving, fill each tuile bowl with the chocolate/ pineapple cream. Dot with a pineapple and chocolate chunk.

ADRIENNE'S SECRET WEAPON...TENNIS

Adrienne and her husband played tennis every weekend when they were at home in New York to stay healthy and help maintain their weight. When they were travelling and eating far more calories than usual it proved to be their secret weapon. It was also a wonderful way to get to know the chefs who plied them with those extra calories since many of them enjoyed the game for the same reason!

Adrienne and Jean Troisgros in The Napa Valley, Nov. 1976
...not sure who won the match but Adrienne's smile gives a clue!

PAMPLEMOUSSE CONFIT

Candied Grapefruit Peel

Jean Troisgros came to visit Adrienne and her husband at their apartment in New York City in 1976. A large supply of grapefruits had just been delivered from Florida. When Jean discovered them he got very excited. "I am going to make you a special grapefruit dish." Adrienne was intrigued. She watched while Jean peeled the rinds off and set aside the fruit. He blanched the rinds repeatedly in boiling water, then reduced them in sugar water. He drained them and sliced the rinds into strips and rolled them in sugar and served them on a plate – Voila! "But what about all the fruit?" Adrienne asked. "Oh, that's for your breakfast in the morning!"

These tart little sweets are lovely as an after-dinner *bonne bouche* and make a great gift at Christmastime. You will find they are still served with coffee after dinner at La Maison Troisgros.

Makes 32

Prep/cook time: 2 hours plus drying time

2 large grapefruit, preferably red, or 4 navel oranges

1½ cups sugar

¾ cup water, or water and grapefruit juice combined

White or Demerara sugar (a light brown, coarse sugar which is not the same as brown sugar)

With the point of a sharp paring knife, score the grapefruit peel into four lengthwise sections. Loosen the peel along with the white pith from the fruit. Place the peels in a 3-quart saucepan, add water to cover, and bring to a boil. Remove from heat. Let stand 10 minutes; drain. Repeat boiling, standing, and draining with fresh water three times. Cool the peels. Cut into strips 4 to 5 inches long and ⅛ to ¼ inch wide.

In the same saucepan, combine the sugar and water (or water and juice from the grapefruits). Bring to a boil, stirring to dissolve the sugar. Add the peels. Cook over medium-low heat, stirring occasionally, for 20 to 25 minutes, or until the peels are translucent. Remove from heat and place the peels on a rack set over wax paper to cool and drain, about 20 minutes.

Roll the peels in the demerara sugar and place on wire racks for several hours or overnight. Store tightly covered in a cool place for up to a month.

IN THE PANTRY

One of the most frustrating situations in the kitchen is to be in the midst of making a recipe and find that you don't have an essential ingredient. You either have to rush out to the store or make a substitution. That's why a well-stocked pantry is essential. I must admit Adrienne was an inveterate shopper when it came to pantry supplies. There wasn't an herb, spice, oil, or vinegar that was safe from her grasp. I don't have her resources but she taught me a valuable lesson: If it tastes, smells, or looks interesting, buy it. You will find a use for it.

SALT

This essential seasoning should be given careful consideration. There are basically two types of salt: rock salt, which is mined; and sea salt, which is produced by evaporation. They both have the same chemical composition; however, the tastes and textures vary and therefore their uses differ as well.

Rock salt is the most common type and is usually encountered as refined table salt, often with added iodine and anti-caking agents. Unrefined rock salt has no additives. Kosher salt is rock salt with no additives but a flat, flaky shape. It is due to its shape that it is used to make meat kosher and therefore acquired the name.

Sea salt comes in fine or coarse grains, or as flakes as in fleur de sel. It does not contain iodine but has various trace elements. Fleur de sel tends to be somewhat moist and, depending on the source, has a distinctive taste.

Unrefined rock salt or sea salt is my preference for cooking, salting water, salting meat, or any other application where it will ultimately be exposed to heat. I use fleur de sel to season food just before consumption. Like extra virgin olive oil, fleur de sel should not be exposed to heat. In addition, it is usually much more expensive than rock salt so should be used judiciously. Many people feel that refined rock salt overwhelms food, but when they switch to the fleur de sel they are astounded by the difference.

SALTING FOOD

Judy Rodgers, the late chef of Zuni Café in San Francisco, was a close friend of Adrienne's. They met in 1973 when Judy was just 16 and spending a year as an exchange student with the Troisgros family in Roanne, France. The food she ate and the passion of the Troisgros family for cooking changed the trajectory of her life.

When she published *The Zuni Café Cookbook* in 2002, Adrienne and I were drooling. We couldn't wait to start cooking her food, which was a lovely combination of rustic French, Italian, and American home cooking. But the biggest impact the book had on us was Judy's use of salt. In almost every recipe, from meat to fish to poultry and vegetables, Judy used salt to deliver flavor, add succulence, and tenderize raw food. We adopted the recommendation to salt early (from 1 hour up to 24 hours in advance) and well (¾ teaspoon salt per pound) for beef, pork, and lamb roasts or chops and whole or cut-up poultry. The result was remarkable. Moist, not salty, food that was delicious. With fish and vegetables, we used less salt (½ teaspoon per pound) for a shorter amount of time (an hour or less). It became a foundation of our cooking. Judy recommends using sea salt, not fleur de sel, but either unrefined sea or rock salt will do the job. I encourage you to get Judy's book and read more about it.

PEPPER

The black peppercorn we are all most familiar with is the cooked and dried unripe fruit of the *Piper nigrum* vine. White peppercorns are the dried ripened fruit. And green peppercorns are the uncooked unripe fruit. Pink peppercorns are a dried berry from an entirely different plant, the *Schinus molle* shrub, commonly known as the Peruvian peppertree, and a relation to the cashew. It may cause allergic reactions in people with nut allergies.

Peppercorns should be purchased whole, then ground in a pepper mill for the best flavor. The black peppercorn has the most assertive flavor. The white peppercorn is more delicate and is often used in butter sauces like beurre blanc with the added advantage that it is less visible while still offering a delicate peppery taste. The green peppercorn can be found fresh or dried. Commonly used in Thai cooking when fresh, it has a bright though mild taste. The classic sauce for venison is made with fresh green peppercorns. Dried green peppercorns lose their bright taste as do the ones in brine. Pink peppercorns have a distinctive taste which is not really peppery but is sharp and can often provide some contrast to sweet dishes, like a strawberry Pavlova made with pink peppercorns in the meringue and on the strawberries.

VINEGAR

There are now as many vinegars available as olive oils. Like everything about cooking, Adrienne always looked for the best quality. This does not mean that expensive vinegar is necessarily better. You really must taste it to determine if it is any good. You should have a variety of vinegars on hand – I keep them in the fridge to prevent evaporation. Basic white wine and red wine vinegars are the starting point. Vinaigre de Jerez (sherry vinegar) is very good in vinaigrettes and tomato salad. Champagne vinegar is lighter and a bit sweeter and can be useful in sauces. Vinaigre de Banyuls was a favorite of Adrienne's for all-around use. Cider vinegar is slightly sweet but very good for adding zing to tomato-based dishes and apple pie. Real balsamic vinegar should be used like extra virgin olive oil, drizzled over vegetables, like the Tomato Salad recipe on page 56, but not on leaf salads. If it is the real thing, it can be quite expensive. Check the ingredients and make sure you are not buying white wine vinegar with caramel coloring added. You won't ever need a lot of it, so buy the best you can and use it sparingly.

BUTTER AND OIL

In all the recipes in this book and all the cooking Adrienne and I have done, we use unsalted butter. Why? Because salt should be added to a dish or sauce in quantities that you control, not hidden in other ingredients.

For frying or sautéing, sunflower oil is our choice. It has a light taste and a high smoking point. Extra virgin olive oil should not be used for frying or sautéing. The delicate, fruity flavor of the oil disappears when it is heated. As it can be quite expensive, you should use it when it's flavor will shine like the tomato salad on page 56 or for dressing vegetables before serving them. Good-quality olive oil (not extra virgin) can be used for sautéing along with an equivalent amount of butter or a mixture of olive and sunflower oil.

WINE FOR COOKING

Cooking wine is not a type of wine but a use for wine. The wine you cook with should always be good enough to drink. White cooking wine generally should be young with a balance that leans toward acidic – a Muscadet or dry Sauvignon blanc is a good choice. For red, a young Côtes du Rhône is our preference. The wine should not be too expensive but obviously, as with all ingredients, the better it is, the better the results. However, as with extra virgin olive oil, a 1961 Crozes-Hermitage should not be used as cooking wine!

HERBS AND SPICES

If you don't have a garden in which to grow herbs, try dedicating a south-facing window as an herb garden. Both fresh and dried herbs have their place in the kitchen and one is not intrinsically better than the other.

You will want to have fresh parsley, thyme, sweet marjoram, oregano, cilantro, tarragon, basil, dill, and rosemary. The rosemary will be a challenge for the window garden because it grows as a shrub, usually in hot, dry climates. It also will not over winter outdoors in northern climes. That and the basil are the only essential herbs that cannot be substituted with a dried version. Many good supermarkets have fresh or potted versions of rosemary and basil. They are usually hot-house grown, but in the middle of winter they are a good alternative.

In most cases, unless specified, the leaves of herbs should be separated from the branches before chopping. This is particularly true with rosemary, thyme, basil, marjoram, and oregano, where the branches tend to be thick and unappealing. But even with parsley and dill the branches can be tough.

In the spice cabinet, well, the world is at your fingertips! I collect spices from my travels and have brought home the North African spice Ras al hanout and wonderful dried rouille from a market in France. Saffron is another one I cannot resist buying, though the cost usually inhibits me!

But let's start with the basics. You will need dried thyme, sage, oregano, and marjoram; even if you have these herbs fresh, the dried versions have different uses and tend to have a stronger taste than the fresh herbs. If you have them in the garden, dry them yourself and store in jars. Bouquet garni sachets are useful when making stock and are available in most supermarkets or gourmet stores; or make your own by tying together fresh sprigs of parsley, sage, and thyme. Bay leaves are also a common ingredient when making stock. The bay tree can easily be grown in a container, which will keep it to a manageable size. Coriander seed and fennel seed are wonderful. The coriander can be used as a substitute for fresh cilantro, and the fennel, with its lovely licorice taste, can stand in for tarragon or basil in some recipes. Cayenne pepper and dried chilis are essential when you want to add a bit of heat. Turmeric and cumin are the basics for Middle Eastern flavors. You might also add za'atar, an unusual, but quite versatile, Middle Eastern herb. It is a relative of oregano and often sold in a

mixture (of the same name) with sesame, sumac, and salt. It is used on vegetables, grilled meat or to season bread. I often use it to add interest to salads. Ras al hanout, the North African spice blend meaning "top of the shop" (indicative of the cost of its many ingredients), can contain up to 100 spices, the primary ones being coriander, cardamom, nutmeg, allspice, cinnamon, and rose buds. It is traditionally used in tagines but is wonderful on any lamb or chicken braise. Chinese five-spice is a similar blend – comprised of star anise, cloves, cinnamon, Sichuan pepper, and fennel seeds – and is brilliant as a rub for chicken, pork, or duck. Finally, the sweeter spices: cinnamon (ground and sticks), ginger (dried and fresh), nutmeg, cloves, and allspice.

OTHER INGREDIENTS

Dried morrilles, porcini, chanterelle, and assorted wild mushrooms are wonderful to have on hand as they can open up a world of possibilities for pasta, risotto, stews, and sauce. Don't forget to save the broth from reconstituting them; it is liquid gold for adding flavor to soups, sauces ,and stews! Liquid hot  sauce is a useful ingredient when you need to kick up the temperature of a sauce or marinade.

EQUIPMENT

It is not necessary to have a state-of-the-art kitchen in order to turn out delicious food, but you do need some essential equipment.

Knives The most important tool in your kitchen is a good knife – actually three: a chef's knife, a paring knife, and a carving knife. Adrienne gave me my first proper knife over 20 years ago. It is a chef's knife with a long wide blade and a beautiful  wooden handle. The blade of the knife is fully embedded into the handle so that it is perfectly balanced. I use that knife almost every day; we are old friends.

Adrienne was obsessive about her knives. She even traveled with them when she went to cook in other people's kitchens. She insisted that you should treat your knives as you would a good friend. Choose them with care and a view to longevity. Treat them well: clean them immediately after using them; don't chuck them in the sink or dishwasher to be cleaned later; sharpen them so that they will always be serviceable. Good knives should not be made of stainless steel because they won't keep an edge.

Pots and pans These are the essentials: cast-iron enamel braising pot, heavy-bottomed sauté pan (a layer of copper between two layers of steel on the bottom of the pan), a saucepan, a copper omelet/sauté pan, a cast-iron skillet, and a nonstick sauté pan.

Food processor This has become a staple in most kitchens. I find it to be such an incredible time saver that I leave it out. If I put it away I find that the effort to get it out means I don't use it as often. We have an architect friend, Lisa, who designed a brilliant cabinet specifically for her food processor. It sits on a platform within the cupboard that you lift out and up on hinges. The platform locks into position at countertop level while you use the food processor and when you are done you unlock it and lower it back into the cupboard. Meanwhile, mine just sits on the counter!

Don't go crazy trying to outfit your kitchen. You can usually punt when you don't have exactly the right dish or pan. Adrienne has been known to use disposable aluminum pans when necessary!

MEASUREMENT CONVERSION CHARTS

U.S. Dry Volume Measurements	
Measure	**Equivalent**
¹⁄₁₆ teaspoon	dash
⅛ teaspoon	a pinch
3 teaspoons	1 tablespoon
⅛ cup	2 tablespoons (= 1 standard coffee scoop)
¼ cup	4 tablespoons
⅓ cup	5 tablespoons plus 1 teaspoon
½ cup	8 tablespoons
¾ cup	12 tablespoons
1 cup	16 tablespoons
1 pound	16 ounces
US liquid volume measurements	
1 pint	2 cups (=16 fluid ounces)
1 quart	2 pints (= 4 cups)
1 gallon	4 quarts (= 16 cups)

Metric to U.S. Conversions	
Measure	**Equivalent**
1 ml	1/5 teaspoon
5 ml	1 teaspoon
15 ml	1 tablespoon
30 ml	1 fluid ounce
100 ml	3.4 fluid ounces
240 ml	1 cup
1 liter	34 fluid ounces
1 liter	4.2 cups
1 liter	2.1 pints
1 liter	1.06 quarts
1 liter	0.26 gallons
100 grams	3.5 ounces
500 grams	1.1 pounds
1 kilogram	2.2 pounds
1 kilogram	35 ounces

U.S. to Metric Conversions	
Measure	**Equivalent**
1/5 teaspoon	1 ml
1 teaspoon	5 ml
1 tablespoon	15 ml
1 fluid ounce	30 ml
1/5 cup	50 ml
1 cup	240 ml
2 cups (1 pint)	470 ml
4 cups (1 quart)	0.95 liter
4 quarts (1 gallon)	3.8 liters
1 ounce	28 grams
1 pound	454 grams

Oven Temperature Conversions		
Fahrenheit	**Celsius**	**Gas Mark**
275° F	140° C	gas mark 1 (cool)
300° F	150° C	gas mark 2
325° F	165° C	gas mark 3 (very moderate)
350° F	180° C	gas mark 4 (moderate)
375° F	190° C	gas mark 5
400° F	200° C	gas mark 6 (moderately hot)
425° F	220° C	gas mark 7 (hot)
450° F	230° C	gas mark 9
475° F	240° C	gas mark 10 (very hot)

INDEX

THANK YOU

Writing may be a solitary endeavor, but in writing this book I was dependent on a wide circle of family, friends, and professionals for support, advice, and encouragement. I am most grateful to Jane Wood for her honest advice and input, which often showed me a path forward when I thought I was against the wall. And to Mindy Dubin and her husband Michael Anthony for their enthusiastic support of this project when it was in its infancy. They kindly introduced me to Dorothy Kalins who was instrumental in finding a copy editor for the book and deciding on the cover. Deri Reed, my copy editor and an absolutely delightful person, added far more value to the book than I ever expected. The two talented artists responsible for the cover and most of the illustrations in the book, Kristina Wheeat and Anna Morozova, delivered results that were well beyond my expectations.

To my children, David and Morgan, family and friends, your love and support got me through the difficult days. For reading and eating this book, helping with social media and marketing, getting your friends and their friends to "like" my page, sign up for the newsletter and, finally, buy the book...I love you and thank you.

Life itself is the proper binge.
— Julia Child

Joan & Adrienne, BFFs forever

Made in the USA
San Bernardino, CA
31 May 2017